THE MARTIN O'NEILL STORY

Anna Smith and David McCarthy

THE MARTIN O'NEILL STORY

Published by the Daily Record, One Central Quay,
Glasgow, G3 8DA.
Copyright: The Daily Record

ISBN 1-901603-14-8

Printed and bound in Scotland

CONTENTS

BIG DAY ... Anthony Martin leads out Celtic against Derry City

Dedication

THIS book is dedicated to the memory of 10-year-old Anthony Martin who died of Leukaemia on the day Celtic clinched the league title. His short life was made special by Martin O'Neill.

ONE

IT WAS a dream that was born in the back garden of a council house.

Fiercely competitive brothers would throw down their jackets for goalposts and live out their sporting fantasies.

Between the clothes poles would be the imaginary stadium - one day a gaelic football park, another day a soccer pitch - where heroes thrilled adoring fans.

And as the boys ran at each other, tackling and dribbling, they would instantly become their idols, ultimately scoring the winner that would bring them world cup clory.

In the midst of this fray was the gutsy young Martin O'Neill, who would amuse his bigger brothers by his tenacious refusal to be beaten.

Looking onto the daily battle of wills was proud father Leo O'Neill delighted at how naturally his fine young sons had taken to sport.

And watching from the kitchen window, their mother, Greta, the driving force behind the family, shook her head, wishing they would spend more time in their books than such frivolous activity as football.

Amid these solid family values young Martin flourished, the sixth of nine children.

He had much to look up to in his older brothers Gerry and Leo and sisters Agatha, Mary and Breedge.

By the time he was seven years old, his brothers had already been through the rigours of boarding school after winning scholarships and his sisters were high achieiving young women.

As Martin's brother Leo, 61, a semi-retired schoolteacher recalled: "There seemed to be this kind of competitive instinct in the family that nothing was ever treated jokingly. Everything became a competition. Nothing was worthwhile unless it was competitive. I never tried to analyse it, because it was just the way we were."

His brothers had already shown great promise in gaelic football which was as much a part of every day life for the O'Neills as going to mass and studying.

Home for the family was an end terrace three-bedroom house in a cul-de-sac in the small farming town of Kilrea tucked away at the edge of County Derry.

Around 40 miles from Derry city and 15 miles from Belfast, Kilrea was far enough away from the growing friction that was to tear Northern Ireland apart in the coming 30 years of the Troubles.

But it was close enough.

And even today, in the busy little town the tricolour that flutters at one street and the union flag at another are reminders that this is still a community split by the sectarian divide.

But whatever was going on across the troubled province, in the O'Neill household the emphasis was on education, sport and competition.

Money was tight, and father Leo, the local barber served the entire communtiy working long hours to provide for his growing family.

Hard work and dedication was bred into the O'Neills for generations as they grew up in a land where poverty often forced the break up of families as siblings trekked the country and beyond in search of work.

Martin's grandmother Bridget Doherty, like many other young women and men, left her native Donegal and went on the 'lagan', the hiring fares where workers were hired for the harvest by farmers offering lodgings and a pittance for months of hard work.

She ended up in Kilrea where she met and fell in love with the local barber Hugh O'Neill and they had seven children including Martin's father Leo, who took over from his father as the town's barber.

Leo described the early years when he and his brother Gerry would come home from boarding school and all nine children were in the house.

He said: "We were poor. But nobody had any money in those days. My mother always had the view that it was important to get us all fed and the rest would come. At least if we were healthy that was the important thing.

"But my mother always coped somehow.

"With some of us at boarding school it was easier because we were getting fed. There were three bedrooms and an adjoining one. There was a living-room and a lounge downstairs that we used as a bedroom. At Christmas and Easter breaks there was a big crowd in the house when we were all there.

"When my father had a business in Kilrea it was not sectarian. We had people from both sides. Our livliehood depended on steering a middle course."

Both Leo and Gerry had left boarding school and were at university by the time Martin went to the college.

When they came home at the weekends the brothers pushed their talented young brother to the limit.

Leo said: "When Martin was growing up, our back garden was sometimes a gaelic pitch, sometimes a soccer pitch and even Wimbledon. On a very rare occasion it was Headingly cricket pitch.

"There was also a big grassy area down the front where we would play, or else on the road. We all played football in teams, and as we grew up it became at a fairly high level."

Their father Leo revelled in sport and was passionate about gaelic football.

Leo said: "Our mother was a very strong driving force in the family, very religious. Martin got his name because of her devotion to St. Martin de Porres. She was the motivational force as far as education was concerned.

"Although we had no money, she was determined that by hook or by crook these children were going to be given the best opportunity she could muster.

"Our father was interested in sport and there was always a fervent support for Celtic in our house. It came from the time that Celtic players used to come to Kilrea. Players like John McPhail, Jock Weir, Willie Miller who played in goals for Celtic, and others used to come and play around Kilrea because some of the Celtic shareholders came from the area. This would be just after the war years and foreign travel wasn't on.

"The boys would frequent my father's shop and they would talk and argue about soccer. I remember them arguing about Charlie Tully, and McPhail saying to my father that as soon as they got him to Celtic park they would teach him a few things. But the following year McPhail admitted they couldn't teach him anything."

As they grew up, competition between the O'Neill boys was furious, and Martin was determined that though his two brothers were at least 12 years older than him, he would match them in any contest.

A story Leo tells, gives an amazing insight into the young boy who simply never knew when to give up.

Leo said: "Martin's hero was Frank Puskas who played for Hungary in the 1960s. My brother Gerry and myself recognised Martin had talent from a very early age and we pushed him on a bit.

"Martin had read in a magazine about Puskas's control of a tennis ball, that he could keep it up for 200 taps without dropping it. So Martin was besotted with this notion that he would have to be able to do it.

"I would go into the garden and after days of practice I would manage about 20 with a tennis ball, then Martin would come in bathed in sweat and say he had done 25.

"This would go on into the next day. I would put the marker up to 50, and my mother used to say, 'You've that wee fella bathed in sweat.' Then Martin would mark it up to 100.

"After a week and a half Martin had accomplished the 200 with ease and I packed it but he kept on.

"So when Martin talks about benchmarks, there is a benchmark there and he was from a very early age a fierce competitor no matter what the sport would be.

"Even when I played golf and he hadn't ever played it, he would beat me because of his putting on the green. His concentration was absolutely immense even as a youngster."

Martin's determination to play in the local parish Kilrea gaelic team brought him to the notice of local priest Father Leo Dearie.

Their friendship has spanned more than 30 years during which time Father Dearie has spent holidays with the family while in England and even married Martin to his childhood sweetheart Geraldine at Nottingham Cathedral.

And when Martin's mother died last year, he asked Father Dearie to officiate at the funeral back in Kilrea.

Father Dearie, now 78, recalled the youngster who pleaded with him to give him a chance even though he was younger than the rest of the team.

He said: "I was in charge of the young footballers and Martin was one of them. He came into the team very young and he was quite small.

"I remember that he was a fantastic player at the time, very keen. I was standing among them once naming the team, the full-back, the half-back, the midfield, and when it came to the forward line he was tugging at my trousers saying, 'Don't forget me sir,'. I named another one or two at the forward line and he kept pulling at me pleading not to forget him, so I put him on as a forward, and one of the other boys said he was too small that he was going to get hurt.

"But I never had to take him off. He played great."

While Martin played at Notts Forest, his future wife Geraldine, a nurse from Kilrea, remained behind. When Father Dearie came home after meeting Martin in England she would be eager for news.

Father Dearie said: "Geraldine was working as a nurse in Derry and would come home at the weekends. She would always make a point of seeing me to ask me how Martin was doing in England.

"I was delighted when I was asked to go over to England to marry them."

Father Dearie added: "Martin was the surprise guest at a celebration in honour of my 50 years as a priest. I didn't even know a do had been planned and when Martin turned up it was brilliant.

"I speak to him from time to time on the phone, and when he got the Celtic job I was pleased for him but worried at the same time because it is such a big challenge. But he is doing so well, and I feel really proud of him."

Martin's arrival at Celtic Park was welcomed by his Glasgow cousin Dan Cassidy who has been a season ticket holder for 23 years.

Born just outside Kilrea in Derry, Dan, now 74, was just eight years old when his family left Ireland.

Dan's mother Bridget died in 1939 when she was only 29 years old leaving her husband to look after five children.

Dan's father worked in the linen industry but as it declined and faced with hardship without a wife, he took his children for a new life across the water.

He was brought up in Rutherglen, but remained close to his roots, visiting the family back in Derry and watching the progress of his young cousin Martin.

Dan recalls watching Martin play gaelic football when he was a boy.

He said: "Martin's older brothers Gerry and Leo were more my age, but I remember his mother taking me out to the back garden when I visited to watch him playing.

"He would be about six or seven and showing real promise."

During the years, Dan was aware of Martin's determination to become a soccer player.

And her remembered giving him some advice, which he is now thankful, that his young cousin ignored.

Dan said: "When Martin was about 18 or 19, Manchester City and some other club were after him and I said to him that he must finish his degree and not to tempted to become a professional footballer which I told him was a very dodgy business. Of course he went on and made a huge success, and I am glad he didn't take my advice.

"I would meet Martin from time to time when he played with Northern Ireland just to say hello to him.

"It's quite incredible that he is now here as manager of Celtic. Leo comes over now for games and we get to spend more time together.

"I have been following Celtic through all the years since 1943 and I am a shareholder. I am very proud of Martin and have been out to watch the team train and have had lunch with Martin.

"He has a real charisma and has got something that football managers should have."

But Martin wasn't the only one to succeed among his brothers.

Apart from Leo who played senior gaelic football in the All Ireland Finals, Gerry took the unknown Armagh gaelic team to the same finals. Owen who came after Martin was a tremendous prospect as a gaelic footballer and youngest brother Shane played soccer for Wolves and even schoolboys international for England much later on. Knee injuries forced them out of sport.

As they grew up, mother Greta always tried to make her children think as individuals. As in all big families there was the odd rebellion, but not from Martin.

Leo said: "When Martin was growing up he had established for himself a code of conduct that didn't necessitate any kind of dictate from our mother or father as to how or what way he should behave. He had programmed himself, with his ethics of living, with his ambition and what he wanted to do. He had all these attributes that he maintained and nourished, but there was a certain element of luck that you require to get on. He had a bit of that as well."

Devoutly Catholic mother Greta had no education herself but firmly believed at an early stage it was the only way forward for people like them in Northern Ireland.

She was determined that her sons and daughters would only achieve anything by education and was anxious that they be given every chance.

Although they could never afford to send their children to the best private schools, all of them won scholarships to grammar school level.

It was against this background all of the family began to emerge as achievers in their own way.

While his older brothers were preparing for university, Martin was to encounter his first hurdle.

After attending his local primary school, St Columba's in Kilrea, until the age of nine, his mother decided send Martin to a primary school across the River Bann into County Antrim where his sister Agatha taught because it had a better reputation while he prepared for the 11 plus exam.

Martin has himself said it was a lonely time for him, having been with one set of school friends since five, then having to start making new friends at a new school.

But it was only the beginning of a much tougher time ahead, where being homesick and lonely built in him a strength of character that was to last a lifetime.

Having won a scholarship to the prestiguous St. Columb's College in Derry city, Martin followed in the footsteps of his two older brothers and became a boarder at the college.

It was a harsh regime of study in a frugal existence which made Martin miserable for most of the time he was there.

St. Columb's has the uniquely historic honour to have produced two nobel prizewinners, namely John Hume SDLP MP for Derry who was instrumental in the Good Friday Agreement, and Irish poet Seamus Heaney.

Composer Phil Coulter was also a contemporary of Martin's when they were there and they have remained friends.

Recently Martin has spoken of his loneliness, of having to come back to Kilrea after weeks at boarding school and feeling like an outsider in his own town.

But despite his unahppiness he excelled in his work and threw himself into sport becoming the rising star in the college gaelic football team.

He captained the Under 14s to the all Ulster youth championships and further glory the following year.

Sean Moynihan, geography teacher and gaelic football team trainer remembered Martin as one of his star players.

He said: "Martin was very skillful, with tremendous ball control and could pass with both his left and right foot. He was very difficult to dispossess once he got the ball and people had to foul him to get the ball off him.

"He was not a tall player, but was very strong, stockily built and with great balance. He had great potential and you could always rely on him during a match to score a goal or two. He was definitely a loss to gaelic football because he was so talented."

Martin's concentration on the game and ability to listen was forged back in those early days at St. Columb's.

Sean added: "He was quite a humble boy and the kind who when you spoke to him tactically about strategy he always took that on board. He was very focused."

While still at St. Columb's Martin played with County Derry minors and went all the way to the All Ireland semi finals.

But it was around this time, in the late 1960s as Martin was preparing for his GCSEs that his family decided to move to Belfast.

At 16, and determined to study to become a lawyer, he had no idea just how dramatically his life would change in two short years.

TWO

AS THE Troubles spread across the province in the late 1960s, the O'Neill's moved away from Derry and Leo got a full time job in a barber shop in Belfast city.

The younger members of the family, Breedge, Martin, Owen, Shane and Roison, all moved to their new home in the relatively quiet area of north Belfast.

The red-bricked two storey semi-detached houses in Kansas and Madison Avenue, were just off the Antrim Road was at that time a peaceful haven close to the Catholic New Lodge enclave and the Protestant Westland scheme nearby.

Settled in Belfast and glad to be back home with his family, Martin thrived at St. Malachy's College the grammar school where he walked into the gaelic football team that was already destined for glory.

In 1970, after months of beating everyone in sight, their team went on to win the coveted Under 19 MacCrory Cup, the premier trophy in gaelic football, bringing the honours back to the St. Malachy's for the first time since 1929.

Their sucess in that took them to the All Ireland Finals where they were narrowly defeated by Cork team from the Colaiste Christu RI school.

It may be over 30 years ago, but to listen to Martin's old team mates and P.E. teacher, it could have been yesterday, as they re-live every moment.

Gerry O'Hare, now 48, and a successful Belfast solicitor, played alongside Martin.

He said: "Martin at that time was the best gaelic footballer I had ever seen.

"The All Ireland Final is remembered more for our defeat than anything. We played the other team off the park and they even came into our dressing room and admitted it after the game."

The following year St. Malachy's reached the Ulster finals in a match that was steeped in controversey.

Martin at that time was also playing soccer for the Belfast Distillery team and the Gaelic Athletics Association frowned upon this, refusing to allow the game to be played in the traditional venue of Casement park.

The St. Malachy's team had to travel up to Omagh for the match where Martin starred alongside his two brothers Owen and Shane who were also making their mark in gaelic football.

The team did not have the normal huge support behind them because of the distance, and the opposing St. Michael's team attempted to psyche out St. Malachy's star player.

Gerry said: "They used to call Martin 'Babyface' because he was so young looking and all of the St. Michael fans were singing the old Al Jolson number 'Babyface' to him whenever he got the ball. But Martin played great."

But St. Malachy's were defeated in the dying moments of the game from a pass that Martin and his team will remember for the rest of their lives.

Gerry said: "All we had to do was to keep possession for the last few minutes. Martin tried to thread a ball through to one of his brothers and it was intercepted by the other team. You knew what was going to happen. Up it went to the other side of the park and they scored.

"We then lost the game, and I remember that Martin blamed himself, which was not the case, but was typical of how seriously he took it.

"After the match he went up to the trainer and said he was sorry about that pass. But it wasn't his fault and nobody held him responsible for it."

Martin's former P.E. teacher at St. Malachy's Brian Molloy, 52, said: "Martin was the most amazing gaelic footballer as a youngster. I watched him in that second match pick up the ball from about

40 yards out and swerve three players just by dropping his shoulder and running past them. Then he fired a shot from 30 yards that dipped and bounced like a table tennis ball into the net.

"No matter how well other players were coached to deal with Martin they never knew when that little jink would come and he would push the ball around them.

"He was never a cocky player and didn't swagger about the park, but he always knew exactly what he was going to do with the ball.

"It is good to watch him coaching now and I am not surprised by his success. I have seen people coaching and no matter how many years they don't make a great success. You have to have something in you, and Martin seems to have that ability to motivate players. I think that is a quality he has had from an early age."

When not playing gaelic football and soccer, Martin was studying and fully absorbed in his plans to become a lawyer.

At St Malachy's he took his studies as seriously as his sport. Martin attained three A-Levels - 'B' in English Literature, 'B' in Latin, and an 'A' in Ancient History. It was enough to take him up to Queen's University with another nine students from St. Malachy's.

His school report before he left gives an insight into the earnest young man who was already showing the stuff of leaders.

Delving into the archives, St. Malachy's headmaster Father Donal McKeown, fished out the buff coloured folder containing Martin's school record.

The glowing tribute said: "He is a popular student arising in part from his prowess in the football field but he also has qualities of quiet leadership which make an influence for good in the college.

"As a college prefect he has shown himself to have a sense of respect and have the welfare of the college at heart.

"He is a pleasant person and is quietly spoken, well principled and in no way spoit by his reputation as a footballer."

The school is proud that one of their old boys has gone on to achieve success.

Father McKeown said: "It is great to have a role model like Martin O'Neill for the pupils here. We have always tried to impress upon the boys that no matter where you come from you can be as good as anyone else if you are determined and work hard.

"We are delighted to watch his success at Celtic and the lads cheer on their team every week."

As Martin and the other boys from St. Malachy's started Queen's University in Belfast, a successful future as a lawyer seemed mapped out for him.

But every moment he had to spare was spent on playing soccer.

THREE

BY DAY Martin O'Neill studied furiously, fascinated by the law.

He would sit through murder trials watching every tactical move of the prosecution and defence as the cases unravelled.

But in the evenings he put aside his law books and pulled on his football boots.

Martin played first for a youth team on Belfast's Ormeau Road called Rosario Youth Club, while he was still a pupil at St. Malachy's.

To this day he still has strong links with the club where his soccer career began when he was just 16 years old.

In the newly refurbished club, the Martin O'Neill trophy room is named after him and brimming with honours won by the young-sters who dream the same dreams that he did.

Rosario youth worker Martin Shiels, 47, who has been with the club more than 30 years, recalls the early days when schoolboy Martin turned up eager for a game with a pal Gerry O'Reilly..

And he tells a story straight out of Roy of the Rovers in a game when Martin turned certain defeat into a massive victory.

He said: "We were in the quarter finals of the Down and Connor Cup and Martin would be about 17. It was in a housing estate called Rathcoole which was about three miles outside Belfast. In those days you didn't have any minibuses to take the team to matches. They had to make their own way.

"On this occasion Martin missed the bus we were all getting from the city centre, and we went up to play without him. We were losing 3-0 at half-time.

"Then O'Neill suddenly turned up and the manager didn't argue too much with him. He just asked what happened and Martin said he missed the bus and he had to get another bus to get there.

"So he went on for the second half and we won the match 5-3. O'Neill scored four goals. We went onto win the final and also the double that year.

"It just demonstrates his leadership at the time. He didn't have to say anything to motivate people, he just went on the pitch and played."

When Martin joined Rosario they were struggling to get a side together and summoned help from the lads at St. Malachy's.

He had to keep his games secret from the Gaelic Athletics Association who would have stopped him playing football if they knew about his forays onto the soccer pitch.

Little did they know that the day before St. Malachy's historic victory in the MacCrory cup, Martin had played soccer for Rosario.

From the beginning Martin Shiels and his team mates knew they had someone special among them.

Martin said: "You knew he was a bit different at the time. His brother Shane also played right through his early days and he was a tremendous player."

After the classic match which took them to the final of the cup, Rosario knew that that the talented Martin would soon be picked up.

It was in the semi-final of that cup that the Distillery team in Belfast spotted the youngster who just wanted to score goals.

But even long after sucess took him to European Cup glory, Martin still follows his old club closely.

Martin Shiels told how he is an icon for the young boys trying to emulate him.

He said: "In the past few days two 11-year-old boys from the club came up to me and asked was it really true that O'Neill really played for Rosario. I think they thought it was all just a club myth, and it really inspired them."

Now with 12 teams ranging from boys and girls up to 18, Rosario is one of the biggest clubs in Northern Ireland, with players from both sides of the religious divide. From time to time Martin re-visits his old club to make presentations and opening tournaments.

Martin remembers one night when O'Neill kept the show going even though there was a powercut at the club presentation night.

He said: "The lights went out in the middle of the evening and Martin said we would just carry on. We took all the kids out to the backyard and he lined them all up and shook hands with them. He spent about an hour with them until we got the lights on.

"He never forgets people either. At that same night a guy came up to him and asked to shake his hand. He said he hadn't seen Martin for 30 years, but Martin remembered his name immediately."

Despite his success, Martin never forgets that Rosario is where it all began.

Martin added: "Martin is a real player's man. He has said to me in the past that if he hadn't played soccer for Rosario he would never have been in soccer. He would never have been picked up by Distillery and then Notts Forest. He's a real gentleman and an inspiration to everyone here."

From youth league success, Martin was clearly head and shoulders above the rest, and the Distillery team in Belfast were one of the first to spot him.

Former Distillery player Alan McCarrol remembers the night Martin walked into the Distillery dressing room.

Allan, who became like a big brother to Martin, recalled: "He was only about 18 and I was about 30. The manager brought him into the dressing room and said to me, 'Would you look after this wee lad.' But he wasn't wee. He was well built and strong.

"Once you saw him playing, you knew by looking at him that he was going to make it. He was very hard to knock off the ball and he had a tremendous strike. He could blast a ball home from 35 yards no bother."

In Belfast at that time, the Troubles were at a height with bombings and shootings commonplace.

The Distillery's club was situated in the city's Grosvenor Road, where one side of the street was Protestant and the other Catholic with banners hanging out of windows during the marching season.

But whatever the naked sectarianism on the streets, inside the Distillery team Protestants and Catholics worked side by side with a committment to each other could serve as a lesson to present day Belfast.

Born and bred in the Shankill Road where he still lives, Allan said: "Religion didn't matter at all to us. Some of us were living in the Falls Road and others in the Shankill, but we all worked for each other. It was brilliant. We were a team who went out and played football and nothing else mattered but trying to make a success of it.

"I still have friends to this day who were Catholics and Protestants who played for the Distillery and so does Martin. I know Martin has respect for all of them."

Allan's friendship with Martin has spanned almost 30 years and they still keep in touch.

He said: "I was in England visiting my son a couple of years ago and I phoned Martin and he insisted I come up to the ground. I was with my family and he made sure we all got fed and got a seat to watch the game. He wanted us to go into the box, but I said we preferred to sit behind the goals. We had a great day.

"Another time when he was in Belfast for the Sportsman of the Year Awards, he phoned me at midnight and insisted I come down to join him at the Europa Hotel for a chat. We sat up until about four in the morning."

Allan recalled when Martin told him last year about the offer from Celtic.

He said: "I thought he seemed a bit unsure, because he knew it was going to be a major step. But I told him if he didn't take the job he would be crazy. I said there were only four football teams to manage in Britain - Celtic, Rangers, Liverpool and Manchester United, and he would regret it for the rest of his life if he didn't take it.

"I also told him he would win the treble, and it looks like he just might."

Martin's goal-scoring ability helped take the team to glory in Ireland and a chance of European success.

He scored two of Distillery's three goals when they defeated Derry City in the Ulster Championships.

Success in that tournament took them into the UEFA Cup where they met Barcelona in round.

They lost 3-1 in the first leg at home, with Martin scoring the only goal. And at Barcelona's New Camp stadium the minnows from Ulster were routed 4-0.

But the moment of playing in front of a crowd of 70,000 fans in Barcelona will remain in the memory of the Distillery team forever.

Another team mate, Roy McDonald, who played in goals with

Distillery and now coaches rivals Crusaders, recalled Martin's early days.

He said: "Having the chance to play in Europe in front of so many fans was a fantastic experience for all the boys. We lost, but Martin played very well. He held his own and was a class act."

Roy recalled the early days when he used to take Martin to and from training at Distillery.

He said: "I remember my father used to drive me to training during the week and we would meet Martin at the bottom of his street. I just remember this wee guy in the back seat of the car not saying too much. He might have been considered a bit dour, but he had a kind of dry wit.

"He was very focused on his football. He knew exactly where he wanted to go and he wanted to be a full time footballer. We all knew he was good enough, but he was never cocky. But on the football pitch he was very confident. He always wanted the ball and he knew what he was going to do with it. Once he had the ball nobody could get it off him.

"When he got the call for Notts Forest we were all delighted for him, because he really deserved it. I did worry a bit because he was a homely kind of boy and I thought he might miss his family too much. But there was a strength there.

"It has been brilliant to watch him develop over the years. He has kept in touch with people down the years and is a great amassador for fooball and Northern Ireland."

Another Distillery team mate, Jim Savage, who scored one of the goals in the 3-1 victory that took them into Europe, said his old pal hasn't changed a bit.

Jim, a 52-year-old school teacher, said: "When I watch Martin on television now it is just like watching the way he expressed himself all those years ago. He was always very precise and chose his words carefully.

He would never boast or brag about anything, but was quietly confident about his ability. He was always very sure of where he was going.

"He brought a lot of his strength from gaelic football into soccer and that made him a powerful player. He was always the one who was earmarked to go further."

When the offer of a chance to play for Notts Forest came up, at just 19-years-old Martin was torn between his career in law and football.

The fee of around £15,000 was a fortune for the club and a

windfall for Martin.

As in all major decisions with the family, all of the O'Neills were summoned to discuss it.

Leo described the scene: "Whenever the opportunity came for a possible move Martin was already established at Queen's University doing law. He had been called up to play for Northern Ireland at one point, and then Forrest came in and expressed an interest in buying Martin.

"There was a general huddle within our family to see what the best thing to do would be, whether to sacrifice the education background which was going to be out of the wiindow, or whether to go into a situation where it was tenuous enough and nothing was guaranteed.

"Our mother was always of the opinion that he should have stuck to his education and the whole question was bandied about between the family for over an hour in the house in Belfast. Martin had been fairly quiet while his future was being decided.

"Eventually my mother asked me what did I think and I said why don't we ask the man concerned. Martin promptly said, 'I want to have a go at the football.' And that was it, there was no further debate.

It was with the confidence of youth that Martin left his country and headed to Notts Forest as a young man full of ambition and determined to make it.

Success followed success, and Martin's parents and younger brothers and sisters followed him to England.

In the early 70s, as the violence on the streets of Belfast spiralled and touched almost every family, Leo and Greta made the agonising decision to uproot their family and make a new life across the water.

At that time the area around the Antrim Road in Belfast was one of the worst for sectarian violence.

In the years that followed the New Lodge area has seen more assassinations than any other part of Northern Ireland.

Leo said: "There was always the off chance that something unforetold could happen. A decision was made jointly that possibly the best was to go to Nottingham, with the younger members of the family and join Martin."

Leo found a job as a warehouseman in Boots factory in Nottingham and he proudly watched his son become a rising star on the field every week.

He delighted at Martin's success, but deep down harboured the lifelong ambition that his son would one day play for his beloved Celtic.

Leo tells of a moment that Martin will remember for the est of his life.

He said: "One of our great heroes was Jock Stein. If Martin ever wanted to emulate anyone at present it would be Stein.

"I remember being with Martin when we met Stein. It was while at Forrest, Martin had been asked to come to Belfast and open a new sporting pavillion along with Jock Stein in Crumlin.

"Stein said to Martin during the evening that he had been interested in signing him at one stage, but at that time they were looking for established players and Martin was still at Distillery.

"It was then that I heard Martin saying to Stein, 'My father always said if ever I got the chance to go to Celtic I should walk all the way to Glasgow.'"

His father never lived to see the dream come true.

Both Leo and Greta died in England, too far away from the back garden in Kilrea where it all began.

Leo was 80 when he died in 1991, and Greta was 86 when she passed away in a nursing home in Nottingham last April.

The family brought her back to Kilrea to be buried alongside their father in the little cemetery.

It was an emotional farewell for two people who out of nothing achieved so much with a family who made them proud.

At Greta's funeral, Martin was already aware of the interest from Celtic to appoint him manager.

Leo said: "Our parents had a sense of achievement as they watched how the family progressed. But father would have had a tremendous sense of achievement had he realised how it would have turned out.

"I remember asking Martin what did he think, and he said to me, 'I would love that.'

"He knew how much it would have meant to our father if he could have been alive to see it."

In the end, he didn't have to walk all the way to Glasgow, but the words of his father are a constant reminder that for Martin O'Neill, managing Celtic will always be more than just a job.

FOUR

THEIR friendship was forged in the gaelic football pitches of a tough boarding school in Derry.

And, almost 35 years on, Dr Raymond White gave an insight into the man who remains one of his greatest friends.

He said: "Martin is like a brother to me. When we meet we hug. There is great warmth between us."

Consultant obstetrician and gynaecologist Dr White recalled the first time they met when 11-year-old Martin arrived at St. Columb's as a boarder in 1953 and he was a day boy.

Raymond said: "It would have been a total upheaval for boarders like Martin coming from the country straight into the regime of St. Columb's. It could be a very harsh regime of studying and strict bedtimes. I think at that time the boarders went months without going home and they were never allowed to go out of the school during the week.

"I sometimes think the strong discipline there was to try to make people strong, though it did break some people."

The boys quickly became close friends, playing gaelic football with the college and later with Derry Minors, as well as running in the same athletics squad.

Raymond said: "Martin has a very dry, very sharp sense of

humour which not everyone appreciates. But he is also quite shy and sometimes people pick that up as a kind of dourness.

"But he can stand up for himself and at St. Columb's he would have to as a boarder or his life would have been more difficult.

"He always talked about the law as a possibilty, but Martin never really declared his hand too much as to what he wanted to do. I always wanted to do medicine, but Martin was always at his happiest with a ball at his feet."

But after helping bring honours to St. Columb's in the gaelic football championships, Martin's family moved to Belfast and they did not meet up again until they both played soccer.

During earlier gaelic matches Martin became one fo the football stars at the school with his famous sidestep which left defenders flat-footed.

Raymond said it was to come back to haunt him when they met up again in soccer matches.

As Martin's team, Belfast Distillery team thrived, Raymond, who was studying medicine at Queen's University, played for their rivals Derry City.

In the cup finals when Distillery beat Derry City 3-1 in May 1971, it was Raymond's job to man mark Martin.

He said: "It was fascinating. I hadn't seen Martin for nearly two years then he suddenly just blasted on the scene as a soccer star with Distillery.

"He was a wonderfully skillful player, very fast and scoring some amazing goals. We played against each other a couple of times.

"The night of the cup final I was marking him but I couldn't get anywhere near him on the pitch. His sidestep came back to haunt me. I was supposed to be marking him but he scored two goals."

The final was played as the Troubles were at a height and very few Derry City supporters turned out. Photographs at the time show the Martin and his team mates doing a lap of honour to an empty stadium at Windsor Park.

Raymond said: "The whole atmosphere of a cup final was affected. Any of the Derry City fans who were there left early and as a sporting occasion for spectators it was sadly not a great event."

After the final, Raymond joined Distillery and they played in the same team that travelled to Barcelona to play in the European Cup Winner's Cup where they were beaten 4-0. In the first leg Distillery lost 3-1 to Barcelona with Martin scoring his team's only goal.

Raymond recalled: "To play in the New Camp stadium was the most fantastic experience in the world. They beat us 4-0 but we really believed it was a moral victory because they had beaten Manchester United 4-0 as well.

"Our tactics at the time was to have 10 men behind the ball and Martin playing up front up front. We had to get the ball up to him, and get him to hold onto the ball as long as possible until we got there.

"Martin was really good, despite our defeat. I remember the next day all the Spanish newspapers were writing about Martin's skill and talent, and they were comparing him to George Best.

"It was unbelievable. I remember us standing at the front desk in the hotel asking the receptionist to translate what the newspapers had said and Martin was a star."

As their careers took totally different paths, Raymond delighted in Martin's success with Notts Forest and Northern Ireland.

In the 1982 World Cup when Northern Ireland beat Spain in Valencia, Raymond joined Martin who had captained the team to victory.

He said: "I was at the match and joined them afterwards in the team hotel and anybody who was there still talks about the celebrations that night, because we had beaten the home nation and moved into the next phase. For Northern Ireland to do that and for Martin to captain them was wonderful."

They have kept in touch through the years, and last year when he was offered the manager's job at Northern Ireland it was Raymond who was to act as the go-between.

He said: "We met in the Europa Hotel in Belfast and talked about it. Martin is always his own man and he makes up his own mind. He has wonderful support in John Robertson who has been with him for years and plenty of friends and advisers.

"But it was nice of him to bounce some things off that aren't too close to him."

Not long afterwards, the old pals met up again when Martin came to the aid of Derry City who were facing financial ruin.

Club chairman Kevin Friel, who had been at St. Columb's with Martin, died in a car crash and the financial mess of Derry City was only discovered after he died.

Facing debts of £180,000 the club was on the verge of being wound up and directors had even put their mortgages on the line to try and save the club.

The courts gave them four weeks to sort out the financial mess.

It was then that commerical director Jim Roddy and Eamon McCourt phoned Martin O'Neill.

Hours before the directors were about to announce to the shareholders they could not find the money, Martin agreed to bring Celtic to Derry for a friendly match which would bring the club much needed finance.

His efforts saved the club from collapse, but as Jim Roddy says, the Celtic visit to Derry did much more than that.

Walking onto the pitch that night to a packed Brandywell stadium was a little boy, 10-year-old Anthony Martin, who had the honour of being mascot for the historic night.

It was to be the best night of his short life.

The fanatical Celtic youngster was suffering from leukaemia and was in remission from the illness when he walked out with his heroes.

But tragically, he died on the Saturday morning before Celtic clinched the league championship.

Jim Roddy, Derry City said: "When Martin heard about the financial ruin of the club he phoned up and spoke to me. I told him that Kevin had died and about the debts which were going to be so difficult to sort out.

"It was the night of a shareholders meeting and I explained the situation to him. He told me to go and tell the shareholders and supporters I am bringing Celtic over and we will all have a good time and help us pull ourselves out of this position.

"I went down and told everyone the news and it was met with rapturous applause. It was massive news, and that was before Martin had done what he has done with Celtic.

"We juggled around dates and finally fixed one for October. We kept the prices down to £15 for seat and £10 to stand. We chartered a plane and flew them into Derry. We put them into a hotel that day and made sure they had everything they needed.

"Martin came on the pitch that night and spoke to the ground and it was unbelievable.

"The last time Celtic were in Northern Ireland there was major trouble in Belfast. This was a real occasion. But there wasn't one iota of trouble.

"Celtic won 2-1. We got Celtic back to the airport and got them away. We didn't want them to stay about the city because it could have been an operational nightmare looking after them. What they did for us was fantastic.

"During the day I know that he went with his old school pals up to St. Columb's and also to the Nazareth House nursing home. There were lots of photographs taken of Martin there with the elderly and I prsented them with the pictures recently. For a group of elderly people it gave them the best joy of their lives."

Jim hopes Celtic will return to Derry in the near future. He said: "I wrote to Martin and I have asked him to bring Celtic back again. After Celtic came, we had Manchester United over after Alex Ferguson heard about our dilemma.

"We have totally turned the debt around and now have money in the bank.

"But what we would like to do is bring Celtic back and give half of the gate money to a charity he would nominate. We would finance Celtic's trip and if there was any money left for us, then fair enough. But the main ethos is to thank the people of the north west who supported us and we would like Celtic to be a part of that celebration.

"Martin O'Neill was the catalyst that saved Derry Football Club from extinction. The club was out of business for 14 years because of the Troubles in northern Ireland.

"In 1985 when Derry went back into business it is well catalogued that rioting stopped that weekend and very seldom does it hit the streets of Derry again. Rioting had been a weekly if not a nightly occurrence before that. "That is what soccer created for Derry and we were in danger of losing that, but Martin helped re-awaken people's passions and make sure that we keep senior soccer in the city."

Jim said that Celtic brought even greater joy to young Anthony Martin who recently died of cancer.

He said: "He had leukaemia and was a mad, fanatical Celtic supporter and his father had come and asked me if he could do mascot for the game. He had been in remission when he walked out that night with all his heroes, but the cancer came back and affected his bone marrown and they could do nothing for him.

"On the day of his wake the boy was laid out on his ed with his Celtic uniform and the picture of Chris Sutton and the team, proud as punch at the top of his bed.

"His father came to me as soon as I walked in the house. He was very emotional and threw his arms around me, and said, that I gave him the best day of his life. But I didn't give him the best day of his life, Martin O'Neill did.

"It is also a way that sometimes people in football don't realise that they do impinge in people's lives, but I honestly believe that Martin understands it because he is a human person.

"Anthony died on the day Celtic won the league. Instead of

bringing the family down a mass card on the lad's body was going to the chapel I took him a Celtic shirt, signed by Martin and the players, that I was given on the night of the match with Derry City.

"I didn't want to give him a wreath or anything because the Celtic shirt seemed more appropriate."

During Martin's trip to Derry, his school pal Raymond said that he was treated like a superstar when he returned to his home town.

And locals couldn't believe their eyes when he turned up in a Derry pub owned by his old college pal Pat Durkin. The great Eusebio had visited the pub when Benfica were in Derry years ago, and Jim asked him to drop in for a picture.

Raymond said: "Everyone nearly dropped their glasses when Martin walked in. It was fantastic. Wherever he went there was a fantastic response from the public.

"Even the night of the match, the loudest cheer of all was when Martin walked onto the pitch."

Martin also took a nostalgic trip to his old boarding school.

Raymond said: "We took him up to St. Columb's and he was like a child. He was running around and pointing out where we played and where he studied. He went into the old dormitories were he slept. But before very long, the headmaster landed in and couldn't believe it. Then the young kids realised who it was and he was mobbed.

"Afterwards we went to Nazareth House where he has an old uncle and the nuns all wanted their picture taken with him.

"The public were so excited at seeing him in Derry that day it was amazing. We had actually to hide him in the back of a car to get him through the town. If he had been spotted he would have been absolutely mobbed."

But one story Raymond tells speaks volumes of just why Martin O'Neill is always remembered by his old friends.

Pat Durkin, who was in the same class during his years at St. Columb's tragically lost his daughter in a car crash in January last year.

When the grieving family looked through her photographs one of them was of Martin O'Neil when he was with Norwich City.

Raymond told Martin and he said he has been wonderfully supportive to Pat.

Raymond added: "Last week before Celtic played Hibs, one of the most crucial matches for them, he spoke to me and wanted to know Pat Durkin's address because he had a signed Celtic jersey, a signed Norwich jersey to give to him as a kind of reminder of his daughter.

"It shows the kind of character Martin. Before one of the biggest matches and yet he was thinking about his close friend in Derry."

FIVE

HE DREAMED the same dreams as his hero Martin O'Neill as he kicked a ball around the garden with his dad.

But10-year-old Anthony Martin didn't live long enough to see his dream come true.

In his short life, as he battled cancer, the youngster showed the kind of courage and determination that puts football and all that surround it into perspective.

And his bravery humbled the big Celtic soccer stars he adored when he walked onto the pitch with them at Derry City's packed Brandywell Stadium last year.

Proudly wearing the Celtic away strip the youngster strode on as mascot to the team he longed to play for.

As striker Chris Sutton noticed the bandage on the boy's arm he asked him what was wrong, and was stunned by the little boy's matter-of-fact reply.

Anthony's dad, Manus Martin, recalled: "Big Chris noticed the elastic bandage on his arm and asked him if he had a sore arm. The wee lad replied, 'I have cancer', and I think Chris Sutton was completely taken aback.

"He immediately asked him to come round to the dressing room after the game."

It is recollections like those that will live in the hearts and minds of Anthony's grief-stricken parents Manus and Majella for the rest of their lives.

It is all they have left of the football daft boy who lived and breathed for the game.

Anthony died hours before Celtic clinched the league championship on April 7

Days after they buried their son, his mum and dad find solace in the bedroom which is a shrine to his beloved Celtic and his TV hero Bart Simpson.

Anthony's Celtic strips hang from his wardrobe, next to his school ties and a signed Celtic ball.

But even with the life size cartoons of Bart adorning the wall, the room has a painful emptiness without Anthony.

This is where he died in his father's arms, just 10 months after leukaemia ravaged his little body and stole away his dreams of being a star footballer.

Tears roll down Manus's face as he remembers how fit and healthy Anthony had been only last May.

He said: "The day before he took ill, Anthony played in a football match with the local team he had been with since he was about six years old.

"Normally all the players would only be on for a short time and would be substituted, but that day he played the whole game. When he came home he was lying on couch and was completely exhausted.

"The next day he took ill in the car. He started to choke and couldn't breathe. I took him to the health centre and we went straight to hospital.

"It turned out to be a tumour that was pressing on his airways and that is why he couldn't breathe."

Non-Hodgkins Lymphoma was diagnosed the following day, but as Majella said, she had a premonition the night before.

She said: "Manus stayed with him in hospital and when he came home he said he was fine and that we would get the results of the tests the following day.

"I told Manus then that I thought Anthony had cancer and I was worried sick. I just knew somehow that something was very wrong."

After the cancer was diagnosed, doctors gave the family hope that with intensive chemotherapy there was a real chance that Anthony would pull through.

Majella said: "We were absolutely shocked. He had been so fit and well. He was always running around with a football at his feet from morning until dark.

"You would look out of the window and he was kicking the ball for his dad to save. That's the way it was every day.

"Now we had to try and take in the news that he had cancer. The doctors at the hospital were magnificent. The consultant sat down with me and Anthony and told him that he had cancer but that we hoped he would get better.

"He took it really well. He seemed to know that he was seriously ill, but he was determined that he would get better."

Two months later he was out of hospital and mid-way through his chemotherapy blocks.

The team he played for the in the quarter finals of a cup tie the night before he took ill had gone onto win the championship, and Anthony was there to collect the honours.

In tears, Manus said: "I remember when the team was going into the final they said to Anthony, 'We're going to win this for you,' and they did.

"I'll never forget seeing him standing there that night. He pulled on a jersey and went up and got his medal. He was so pleased."

The treatment had dissolved Anthony's tumour and the chemotherapy appeared to be working.

It was in October when Martin O'Neill brought Celtic over for the friendly match to help turn around Derry City's finances, that Anthony was given the best night of his life.

His dad had asked Derry City's commercial director Jim Roddy if Anthony could be a mascot for the historic night, and Jim, aware of the boy's illness, immediately agreed.

Majella recalled: "We were so thrilled to get a ticket at the last minute to see Anthony walking onto the pitch. He had a smile from one ear to the next. I've never seen him so happy."

Manus said: "It was marvellous. I had taken Anthony to a match at Celtic park a few years ago and he was thrilled by the whole occasion. When I saw him walking on with all the players that night I knew that this was the happiest day of his entire life.

"Chris Sutton told him to come round to the dressing room after the match but it was too cold and I wanted to get Anthony back home."

The night had made Anthony the happiest little boy in the world. The leukaemia seemed to be under control and his family were looking forward to Anthony's final batch of chemotherapy.

But just three months later, he suffered a relapse.

As he was about to begin his final block of chemotherapy, a lumber puncture test showed that the cancer had spread through to his bone marrow and it was so virulent that the medication was not working.

From January, Anthony went downhill very quickly.

But despite his failing health, he and the other cancer children at the Royal Belfast Hospital's haematology unit in Belfast kept medical staff spirits up.

Manus said: "There were another two boys from Derry in with cancer and Anthony and the others used to describe themselves as the wee sexy men from Derry. That's what they became known as in the ward and everyone used to kid them.

"He would always say, 'Goodnight, God bless...I love you, best mammy in the world...' as his last words whenever we left him. No matter what we were talking about, those were always his last words. Anthony showed amazing spirit. He used to tell us that we worried too much.

"He was Celtic mad. We would be watching a match on television and I would be getting annoyed and would maybe even swear a bit. Anthony knew that he wasn't to swear, but I allowed him to if he was watching a match. He used to say to me, 'Can I swear now daddy?,' and we would laugh.

"When the doctors told us that there was nothing more they could do for Anthony we knew the end would be fairly quick.

"After the initial shock we decided to make it the best we could for him for his remaining time with us.

"There had been a plan for some time to take him to the Celtic v Dundee United game in March through the Belfast charity Shine A Light, but when the time came he was too ill to go."

Majella and Manus, along with their daughter Kate, nine, watched as Anthony lost his battle for life.

He was sent home from hospital to be with his family for the final days.

Majella said: "He was the most patient, understanding little boy anyone could ever imagine. He would never complain about the cancer. Now and again he would ask for something to take the pain away, but he never asked to take the cancer away. He use to apologise if he was too tired to talk to visitors.

"I sometimes thought that he knew deep down that he was dying and I wondered if he understood it. The house was full of people coming to support us and visit the family and I think Anthony must have known something.

"I remember one day just before he died, he called myself and Manus into the room and put his arms around us. He said, 'I just wanted to give you a hug.'

"Manus thinks that he knew he was dying and that he wanted to say goodbye to us."

Manus said: "I remember a couple of days before he died, his school pals were in visiting him and he wanted to see them off. I got him ready and I was heartbroken as I saw him shuffling around like an old man at 90. The cancer was right through his bones, but he wanted to wave his pals off. He didn't want his pals to see him like this. That was the kind of boy he was."

During the weeks before his death, Manus contacted other cancer families on the internet, and messages of support as well as toys flooded in from all over the world.

When the end came, it was as Manus held Anthony in his arms, with Majella talking to him.

Majella said: "I had been told by another family who had lost their child to cancer that I should speak to him, even if he appears to be lapsing in and out of consciousness.

"I just spoke to him for about 25 minutes, telling him how much I loved him and how much we were all going to miss him."

Manus said: "I held him in my arms until he stopped breathing."

It was the Saturday morning hours before Celtic beat St. Mirren to crown them league champions.

With tears blinding him, Manus dressed his son in his Celtic shirt and lay him on the bed, surrounded by photographs of his Celtic heroes.

He said: "After Celtic won the championship I went upstairs and told Anthony the news. I knew he would have been so happy if he had lived to see it."

Jim Roddy of Derry City, who visited the family the following day, said: "When I went to the house after Anthony died, Manus put his arms around me and cried. He said that I had given Anthony the best day of his life by giving him the chance to be a mascot with Celtic that night.

"But it was Martin O'Neill who gave the wee boy the best day of his life by bringing Celtic over here."

Just before the undertaker put the lid on Anthony's coffin, his dad slipped a pair of trainers on him, "in case there was a football game up in heaven."

And even at his funeral, Father Fintan Diggin spoke of Anthony's love of Celtic.

Manus said: "The priest said that there was no way that Celtic could lose the championship in the match against St. Mirren because they had a 12th man on the park that day.

"Every time I watch Celtic now I will be thinking of Anthony watching over them and willing them on. He will always be their 12th man.

"I just wish he could be here to share it all with us."

The children's haematology unit at the Royal Belfast Hospital is the only children's cancer unit in the whole of Northern Ireland.

All newly diagnosed children with cancer, whether it is from tumours or leukaemia are referred and undergo treatment there.

The eight-bedded unit sees the 40 to 50 new child cancer cases from babies to 16 year olds that are diagnosed in the province each year.

Much of the treatment, once they are diagnosed is outpatient chemotherapy.

Like every hospital unit, much of the funding comes from charity some of it from grateful patients.

Manus and Majella would like to see a room where people can have some privacy while they either wait for treatment or simply try to come to terms with the sheer difficulties they are facing.

Cash is also needed for equipment as well as supporting educational courses for staff, and the unit generally.

Dr McCarthy: "Anthony was a real character. He always had something to say for himself.

"He was really terribly unwell when he came to us last May with a very large lesion in his chest which was causing breathing problems.

"Following treatment he responded very well which resolved a lot of his symptoms, and then his real character came out.

"He was a Bart Simpson addict and everything he did revolved around that.

"He was also Celtic mad and he used to show me pictures of all his heroes. He was really proud of that day he led them onto the pitch at Brandywell as the Celtic mascot, and he had all the photographs to show off to people.

"He got an awful lot of strength from his parents. His mum and dad were great. They were an inspiration to the unit whenever they came in, always getting involved with other families and full of joy and chat.

"Anthony was almost stoic in everything we used to say to him.

He almost tried to obviously ignore what we were saying and didn't appear to give the impression that he was listening. But in the same breath, his mother told me later, that he knew well what was going on.

"He would know by the change in attitude of me and others unconsciously had towards him. Most children aged as he was would be well aware that things are not going as well as they should be.

"Most children don't really deal with death. It is something a long way away and they only deal with the here and now and Anthony was very much like that.

"But when any child dies in the unit who you have watched for a long time people in the unit are deeply affected by it. We deal with it in our own way.

"Some children you can get closer to than others. Everyone was very fond of Anthony.

"His parents are finding it terribly difficult to cope. Anthony was their shining star and he has now left. They have dedicated themselves to fund raising for the unit and that is very laudible. A lot of parents get themselves inolved in something so that they can live from day to day.

"The idea of dedicating the book to Anthony lovely and I know that it will help them in their grief."

SIX

A PSYCHOLOGIST would have a field day trying to analyse the relationship between Martin O'Neill and the man most widely regarded as his mentor, Brian Clough.

O'Neill insists the legendary Nottingham Forest manager neither liked nor rated him, preferring the more aesthetically pleasing talents of John Robertson on the other wing.

There might be some truth in that assertion, or it might be simply O'Neill's well worn line in self deprecation, but the facts don't bear out the paranoia. If that's what it is.

After all, Clough picked O'Neill on more than 200 occasions for Forest.

The player won two European Cup medals - although he was left on the bench for the first of Forest's two finals in 1979 - a league championship and two League Cup medals under the irascible management of Clough, which tends to suggest that the master did have a degree of admiration for the pupil. Even if he didn't lavish him with praise.

There were, though, instances when O'Neill looks as if he had a point. Take the 1978 Charity Shield at Wembley. Forest are stuffing Ipswich Town 4-0 (it ended 5-0) and O'Neill has just scored his second goal of the game.

A cherished Wembley hat-trick is on the cards but Clough makes a substitution and it is O'Neill who is told to come off.

In the official history of Nottingham Forest, O'Neill takes up the story.

He said: "I asked him why he'd taken me off and he replied: 'Because you're crap and you always will be crap.'

"I'm not sure he knew exactly how to get the best out of me."

An even harsher blow was O'Neill's omission from the Forest team that lifted the European Cup for the first time in 1979. The Swedish side Malmo were in opposition and Forest were hot favourites to lift the trophy in Munich.

They let no-one down, winning the match 1-0, but O'Neill had been injured and although he claims he was fit to play in the final, Clough left him on the bench.

He did, however, play in the final the following year when a 1-0 win over Hamburg in Madrid saw Nottingham Forest retain their trophy – an astounding feat for a provincial English club.

O'Neill recalled: "The Hamburg game was enormously important to me because I had only been on the bench against Malmo.

"It had been my boyhood dream to do what Puskas and di Stefano had done and it was incredible that I could do this thing.

"It was very important to play well because Hamburg was one of the few games Brian thought we could lose.

"It is possible that I was rather more paranoid than most of the team. John Robertson never used to worry too much, but then he was the key to the whole thing.

"I used to spend my time worrying because I felt that if the team played badly, I would be the one he would drop.

"They say that only the paranoid survive but I suppose I couldn't have been that bad because I played in 38 of the 42 games we went unbeaten in one year and 38 of the season we won the championship.

"I wanted to play in central midfield but I only got one chance to do that, when we beat Barcelona in the Super Cup Final and I played really well.

"But we got off the pitch and Cloughie said: 'Don't worry, when John McGovern's fit, you'll be back on the right again.

"Going back to the Malmo game, I was injured three weeks before the final but I was fit to play in the game.

"Cloughie called Archie Gemmill, Frank Clark and myself over to one of the corners and asked: 'Are you all fit?'. We all said yes, of course. 'You're all lying and I can only risk one of you,' he said and he chose to risk Frank. I don't think Archie ever forgave him.

"The sense of loss for me was immense because I was convinced we couldn't lose and I was being denied a European Cup winners' medal.

"So when we got to the final the following year, not to have played would have been heartbreaking."

O'Neill did play, though, and a goal from his long-time pal and current Celtic assistant John Robertson won the trophy for Forest.

By that time, another medal was in the cabinet - the League Cup was won in 1979 - but only after a management ploy that could only have come from Clough.

O'Neill added: "Cloughie kept us up drinking until 1.30am the night before the game. Heaven knows what he was thinking about.

"Robbo and I ended up carrying Tony Woodcock upstairs and we were absolute garbage in the first half against Southampton.

"We went into the dressing room 1-0 down and Cloughie just looked at us. 'Don't any of you dare suggest that performance had anything to do with last night,' was all he said.

"So we all just sat in total silence for 10 minutes and went out and won the game 3-2. Gary Birtles had an outstanding game and scored twice.

"When I was managing at Wycombe I tried the same thing myself at Runcorn. All I got for it was a splitting headache and a six-goal thrashing."

There were other events that non-plussed and frustrated O'Neill. Like the time Clough told him there was no point in giving him the ball because there was a genius on the other wing.

The Irishman claims his manager only praised him twice in his entire playing career. But he admits that only at the end of the tempestous relationship did O'Neill really appreciate Clough's own brand of genius.

He added: "I don't think I appreciated what Brian Clough achieved as a manager until afterwards when I was able to make comparisons with other managers. It was only then that I could see that he was a class apart.

"Obviously, like most players at the time, my thinking was sub-jective and not objective and my interests were my success - whether I was in the team and not so much was good for the team.

"It's probably true to say I argued with him rather more than any of the rest of the squad.

"When I think about it now, all I ever really wanted from Brian was for him to say: 'You did really well out there...'

"If we'd have been playing in front of 40,000 and they all thought I was manure it would not have worried me at all if Brian had praised me afterwards.

"But you would have had to be really bone stupid to be with Brian Clough for five or six years and not learn something about the art of management.

"Everything was plain and simple, especially when you are being told off which only happened to me about 15 times a day.

"I learned an awful lot from Brian Clough. I also learned from other managers that I didn't have fantastic respect for, even if it was how not to do the job.

"You've got to be yourself and I am my normal cantakerous self. I don't spend my life wondering how people greater than me would approach a problem. I have to approach it myself. A lot of it is gut feeling, to be honest."

Clough demanded complete autonomy to run Nottingham Forest as he saw fit. It is one of the traits O'Neill has followed.

The Celtic manager said: "There's a feeling now that a coach is exactly that. He looks after first team affairs and that's it really.

"Well, I don't see that as my role. That is the most important aspect of it, of course, but I believe I am the manager of this football club and that it does need managing. Until someone tells me I'm not doing that well enough I'll try to get my ideas across.

"I'm not delving into everybody and telling them how to do their jobs but I don't want anybody telling me how to do mine because I actually know it better than most people."

Now that's the kind of talk that would bring a smile to Brian Clough's face.

SEVEN

BRIAN CLOUGH allows himself a knowing smile. After all, he always insisted Martin O'Neill would make it as a manager.

Clough didn't get much wrong in football management and eight years into his retirement it doesn't look like a lot has changed.

He might be 66-years-old now and time has taken its toll on features that look more frail with each passing month but the man who nurtured and nagged O'Neill through the most successful spell of his playing career is a contented individual.

Clough can wrap the memories of winning two European Cups with Nottingham Forest and two league championships – one with Derby County – around him like a warm winter coat and on the day we meet he might just need it.

A cold wind slaps at the face but as we move into his friend's home just a mile from Clough's own mansion in a quiet village on the outskirts of Derby, the handshake is warm and welcoming.

For a man who had a reputation as a journalist-basher, it seems Clough has mellowed.

Of course, we are here to speak to about a subject that is obviously close to his heart, even if that was not always the case.

Clough now considers himself to be a friend of O'Neill but he concedes that the relationship had to survive more than a few rocky passages.

The Irishman had been at Forest for two years before he arrived in 1974 and Clough's first impression was that this young man was a know-all who needed to be taken down a couple of pegs.

Clough was just the man to do it but the picture he paints of O'Neill, while not always the most flattering, is one of many layers.

The manager realised that beneath the brash exterior, there lay within the young O'Neill an all-consuming desire to learn every nuance of the game.

They had their disagreements and on one occasion Clough came close to stripping O'Neill of his most cherished achievement in the game – his European Cup winners medal – after a breach of discipline.

But after the rows came the respect. O'Neill has won it from Clough and few have done that. He may well regard that as one of his greatest achievements.

There's a twinkle in Clough's eyes as he casts his mind back to life with Martin in the six years they shared at Nottingham.

"In the early days with Martin everything was a battle with him," he said.

"He wouldn't play the way I wanted him to. I used to say to Martin: 'You should have played a game that involved two footballs – one for you and one for the other 10.' He always wanted to hold onto the ball and I wanted him to play it.

"I was always saying to him that it was a simple game. Get the ball, control it and give it to one of your colleagues. I didn't want him running 30 yards with the ball and losing it because that's what would have happened.

"I used to pass him going to the dressing room and throw a ball at him: "Go on, play it,' I'd shout. 'It's round – its meant to be passed.'

"The ultimate way to get it across to him was at Wembley in the Charity Shield when we played Ipswich and murdered them. We were winning 4-0 in the second half and Martin had scored two and was looking for his hat-trick.

"I turned to Jimmy Gordon on our bench and said: 'If O'Neill doesn't play the ball the next time he gets it, I am pulling him off.

"Jimmy laughed and said: 'Not even you would do that when someone is going for a Wembley hat-trick.'

"Next time he got the ball, he didn't play it and I got Jimmy to hold up the board with his number on it. Martin was on the far side of the pitch and he couldn't believe it. It took him about three days to walk off."

Clough laughs as he tells the story. He is clearly enjoying the memory. He wasn't so happy in the aftermath of another cup final. The big one. The European Cup Final of 1980.

Forest, who had beaten Malmo to the trophy 12 months earlier, won it for the second successive season, defying the odds to beat Hamburg with a goal from John Robertson.

Clough takes up the story: "We had our ups and downs. I left him out of the European Cup Final in 79 although I think he's forgiven me now. We are now good friends but it took a long while.

"I left him out because I knew he was injured and he said he wasn't. Archie Gemmill was the same, so he didn't play either. They were both legends in their own countries but that didn't matter to me.

"It was an hour before kick off and we'd being doing some light training – we didn't do much before games, just messed about really – and I asked Martin how his hamstring was.

'Right as rain came the reply.' I just said: 'You're not playing Martin and neither are you, Archie.' I know they were devastated and angry but it had to be done. They never said a word to me, they just walked away.

"They played in the second one though and they were brilliant. Maybe missing the first one had that effect on them. We had to be good because the Germans were better than the Swedes the year before.

"Martin revelled in it and his pal scored the winning goal. I won't say they gave 101 percent because that's a load of bull. There's no such thing and if they had not given me 100 percent every week they wouldn't have been in the team in the first place.

"Winning the trophy was a magnificent achievement for a club of Nottingham Forest's size. To have done it once was fantastic, but to defend the European Cup as we did was unbelievable. Except we all believed we could do it even if nobody else did.

"But there was a bit of bother even after that game. A group of our players were disappointed when I imposed fines on them before we'd even set off home with the trophy.

"We had tucked ourselves away in a hotel miles out of Madrid, but the players' wives and girlfriends were staying in the city and after the match several of the players asked if they could go into town and join them.

'Not a prayer,' I told them - and despite heated attempts to persuade me to change my mind, I refused.

"I said: 'We came together as a team and we stick together as a team. I don't want you pissing off into town or anywhere else. We've won the European Cup and we'll celebrate together.

"But some of the group – O'Neill, Robertson, Larry Lloyd and Kenny Burns I seem to remember – made up their own minds to defy my orders.

"When I found out I was so incensed that I decided to confiscate their European Cup winners' medals. Can you imagine the outcry that would have caused back home?

"I gave the matter a lot of thought but finally opted for fining them a few quid apiece. John Robertson as well – you don't bend the rules, not even for heroes.

"We had unwritten rules. People thought I ran it like a concentration camp but it wasn't like that.

"We'd sit down and discuss what was acceptable. I'd tell them I didn't want them pictured at 4am with a pint in their hand. They knew that if they got into bother they'd get done by me, so there was no excuse.

"But Martin wasn't much of a drinker. He was a half of lager man. John Robertson would have just a little bit more. Just about enough to have sunk the Titanic."

O'Neill would continually bend his manager's ear about the favouritism he claimed Clough showed towards Robertson, while he was at the back of the line when the plaudits were being handed out.

The managerial legend smiles at the recollection. He said: "I think people thought Robbo was my son, while Martin was the black sheep of the family – someone I hid away in the attic.

"It wasn't like that, of course, but I knew it wound Martin up and I used to play on it a little.

"Very few people realise just how good a player Robbo was. He was fat and he was short, but give him the ball at his feet and an inch to cross it and he would put it into the danger area.

"He wouldn't run back when we didn't have the ball. I kept telling him: 'Robbo, the halfway line doesn't move towards you – you have to move towards it when we don't have the ball.'

"But he was brilliant. I just said to the players: 'When you are in trouble, give the ball to Robbo. You know where he'll be because the lazy bugger never bloody moves.'

"Martin used to score more goals than John and couldn't understand why Robbo was my favourite," he recalled.

"I used to upset him by saying he only got so many goals because Robbo was doing all the hard work by delivering the ball into the area for Martin to score.

He would say: "You don't like me.' I would say: 'You are right – I don't like Catholics, I don't like coloured people and the Jews get on my nerves'. I didn't mean it but I knew it would annoy him."

Despite feeling that he wasn't getting the recognition he was due, O'Neill didn't let his feelings colour his friendship with Robertson.

They were separated by the width of a pitch on match-days but off the field they were rarely found apart.

Brian Clough accepts that O'Neill and Robbo are complete opposites and always were. And while he had to work hard at liking Martin in the early days, he took an instant shine to the rogue that was Robbo.

Clough said: "I know Martin goes on about Robbo being my favourite son and that I didn't care much for him. He was possibly right.

" You couldn't help like Robbo, even if he was a tramp. He always had suede shoes that were covered in chip fat. I used to say the binmen would refuse to take them away if he put them out.

"But for all that, and for the fact that he was a lazy sod, Robbo could play.

"He and Martin were complete opposites but they were great pals.

"Even before I got to the club they were mates. They came into the side together, they roomed together and both learned their trades together.

"They gelled on the field because they were opposites style-wise. Robertson didn't have to be told to play the ball, it came automatically, while Martin would want to touch it five times.

"When I brought all these so called stars in, those two would give them stick by saying: 'We built this club before you came.'

"They hadn't, of course, but I liked my players to have a bit of cheek and they had that."

O'Neill had a little too much cheek for Clough's liking on occasion.

He said: "He used to tell me that he might as well go back to university because I wasn't giving him a chance. I stood it for a long time, then one day I had enough.

"I said: 'Mention that one more time and I will have you on the next boat back to where you belong - even if I have to hire it and pay for it myself.

"He didn't mention it again. He was an intelligent boy and he was no trouble as a trainer. He didn't carry any weight, which helped. His mouth would never stop working, but neither would his legs.

"He would have quiet spells when he twigged there was no merit in arguing. He would start off questioning things, saying: "What are we doing this for?' I'd say: 'Cos I'm ******* telling you.'

"I would ask him things to wind him up. 'Where's the most bones in your body, Martin?' and he'd say: 'I don't know I'm not a doctor.' I'd say: "Ah, so there is something you don't know. That's interesting.'

"And I used to tell him that he'd go bald because he headed the ball on the top of his head instead of his forehead. He was no Tommy Lawton, that's for sure. Have a look at his head now, he's losing his hair. Maybe I was right all along."

Through all the disagreements, however, Clough recognised and admired the fire that burned brightly within O'Neill. He still does.

He said: "I knew he'd be a manager. He wanted to learn and he wanted to talk. He wanted to analyse and he wanted to steal ideas. He'd do anything. He would put up with me because he wanted something from me - he drained me but he did it nicely.

"If you lot in Scotland think he chunters on a bit, you should have heard him at Forest 20 years ago.

"You talk to him for an hour then you go home shattered because he's talked at you so much. Your ears are knackered and he's wanted to know everything."

That said, however, Clough is delighted that O'Neill was not given the opportunity to fill his trainers at the City Ground after he resigned in 1993.

The Irishman was climbing the managerial ladder with Wycombe and had already established a reputation as a young boss with a big future.

But Clough ferverently believes that trying to replace him at Forest would have been a major mistake at that stage in Martin's managerial development.

He sits back in his chair, the fingertips of both hands touching and forming a triangle, purses his lips and finally says: "It wouldn't have been right for him to have followed right after me at Forest – and that's not me being Old Big 'Ed again.

"With all the success I'd had it would have been impossible for any young manager to try to emulate that, and Forest at the time were beginning to slide.

"No, I was glad he wasn't given the Forest job when I left in 1993. It would have been too soon for him and it would not have been easy for him. He did it the right way. He learned his trade with non-league clubs then Wycombe and Leicester.

"I don't know if he has taken on my management style because he is his own man.

"I don't go into the dressing room with him but I would imagine that having been brought up under me, he is not afraid to speak his mind to players. He can talk, and he is bright enough to articulate himself to the players. Not every manager can do that.

"If he's learned anything from me, it is probably how to stand up to situations. Sometimes football is not easy. You lose, you can be tired and you are disappointed. But he knows what to say to players in those situations and he gets things off his chest rather than bottling them up.

"I do hope that his team laughs, though. We had a team that laughed at Forest and I am sure that the players at Celtic will laugh.

"They will certainly listen."

The Celtic boss turned 49 on March 1. Clough believes he is at an age where good managers should be looking to become great managers. He insists O'Neill is on the verge of making the leap.

"He's in his late 40s now and approaching his peak," said Clough.

"I approached mine at an earlier age but then again I was in management earlier and I'm always telling Martin that I had the won the league championship by the time I was 39 and the European Cup twice by the age of 45. The young man still has some way to go.

"But he has retained his enthusiasm for the game, he wants to be an excellent manager and he is under no illusions about the difficulties the job entails.

"He was a certainty to go into management and he will get better.

"In the next couple of years he'll be over 50 and he might not be able to do as much on the training ground, so he will draw on what he's learned and he'll use that experience wisely."

O'Neill invited Clough and his wife Barbara to the 1999 Worthington Cup Final at Wembley. They haven't met since but the master hopes the apprentice asks him to Scotland in the near future.

He added: "He gave us both a kiss that day, as I remember.

Barbara enjoyed it more than I did. I haven't seen him since but I've been watching what he is doing.

"Maybe he'll invite me up for the end of season bash. I go to Cala Millor at that time every year, but I can always fly from Glasgow. The last time I was up there, I couldn't believe how beautiful it was. It's changed for the better and I'd love to go back."

If and when he does, he may be surprised at just how deep O'Neill has embedded himself into Celtic's folklore within a year of arriving at Parkhead.

Derailing so spectacularly the Rangers bandwagon in his first season has made the former Leicester City manager a hero forever in the eyes of the legions who live and breathe the club .

Clough believes, however, that O'Neill will be using this season as a launchpad for future success at home and in Europe.

He knows that many will scoff at the notion, but the former Derby and Forest manager believes that Martin could even add the title of European Cup winning manager to that of European Cup winning player to his CV given time.

He added: "He is already achieving great things at Celtic – it'll have been a long time since they were so far ahead .

"He'll be under pressure in the Champions League but it'll be a nice pressure. He'll be able to take the players away for a few days before each game and they'll enjoy that.

"I used to use that thought to motivate the players. I'd tell them, go out and win this game and just think, we'll be off in the next round to a sunny place where they could take the golf clubs or lie on a beach.

"We used to treat the European trips like a holiday with a game thrown in. Maybe Martin will do that as well."

"Now that he's won the league, he'll have to do it again. I see him jumping up and down when Celtic score. Next season I want to see him jump higher. I want to see that he is even more determined next season. I want to see signs that he's learned from his first season in Scotland and that he is still improving as a manager. I am sure he will.

"He can win the European Cup with Celtic. He really can. I have no doubt about it. Other people might, but they said the same thing about Forest and we did it twice and when I was at Derby we got to the semi final and were only robbed by a bastard referee who had been bought.

"His future at Celtic depends on whether he is happy. I am sure he is at the moment but management is a lonely business irrespective of who you have around you.

"He might get linked with moves to Manchester United or other big clubs in England, but if he is happy he will stay. He knows he's good enough for Scotland but there is a big pool next door and he might want to test himself in it again some time."

That's why, Clough insists Celtic's board of directors could do themselves a real favour by sitting down with O'Neill and thrashing out a long term contract that will give him the stability he needs to see this job through.

With typical bluntness, O'Neill's mentor continued: "I don't know who the Celtic chairman is and I'm not interested. But the most important decision that man will ever make is getting Martin to sign a long term contract. That should be his first and foremost job. If Martin hadn't gone to Celtic, they'd still be average.

"What else have directors got to do with their time? They'll be sitting there thinking about where to install mens and womens toilets in the ground, when they should be getting Martin tied up.

"They should do it now. They should say to him, how long do you want the contract to be and how much do you want paid. Unless Martin says something daft like £1m a week, they should have him signed up by Christmas."

O'Neill might have been know-all in the glory days of Forest but there's one thing he didn't know, still doesn't and never will.

Clough smiles: "He wants my phone number, but he won't get it. Nobody gets my phone number, young man."

EIGHT

MARTIN O'NEILL extols the virtue of patience among the members of his squad who cannot get a regular game at Parkhead.

But the Celtic manager admits he didn't always practice what he preaches.

It might have been almost 30 years ago but O'Neill still remembers, somewhat cringingly, the day he demanded a move from Nottingham Forest because he wasn't getting first team football.

By his own admission, Martin wasn't short of confidence when he hit the British mainland for the first time as a 19-year-old from Northern Irish football.

In fact, the kid thought he'd made it because Forest, who were in the old English Second Division at the time, had signed him. He was in for a shock.

O'Neill said: "I know from my own experience as a player that the important thing is that you have confidence in your ability so that whoever the manager may be you will be at the forefront of events.

"But it can't always happen like that. I remember my early days with Nottingham Forest.

"Matt Gillies was the manager who brought me over. He was a

very fine man and I thought: 'He's bought me so he must think I'm a great player'.

"Of course, that lasted for about a week.

"I got into the first team quite early after coming from Irish football and – amazingly – I got left out after a game or two!

"I was so big-headed I thought: 'How can he possibly leave me out of this team?'

"There I was, asking for a transfer within six weeks of arriving at the club. I cringe with embarrassment when I think about it now."

O'Neill might just have become another statistic – a promising young import who failed to make the grade – but for the sacking of the man who had paid £15,000 to bring him from Ireland.

Gillies was replaced as manager by legendary Scottish midfield player Dave Mackay, who rated O'Neill far higher and reinstated him to the first team.

The transfer request was withdrawn and Martin went on to win a League Championship, two European Cups and two League Cups before leaving the club in 1980.

But Mackay stayed for only season and his replacement, Allan Brown, wasn't a Martin O'Neill fan as the Celtic boss later recalled, saying: "My career blossomed under Dave Mackay and it was a massive blow when left to go to Derby County.

"A new manager came in, Allan Brown, and didn't fancy me one bit.

"I was in and out of the team at that time, always blaming the manager, and, of course, never blaming myself. Anyone who was prepared to listen would be told the manager doesn't play my style of game and that he didn't know one footballer from another.

"The truth of the matter was that I didn't look closely enough at myself.

"When the next manager, Brian Clough, came in he forced us all to look at ourselves and reappraise our ability.

"Myself, John Robertson – who was a fantastic footballer – and Tony Woodcock were drifting. We were going nowhere but we all thought we were great. The truth is that we weren't."

Eyal Berkovic would maybe recognise where O'Neill is coming from with these words but it is doubtful. The little Israeli playmaker has talent all right, but his unwillingness to adopt the work ethic demanded by the manager has left him out in the cold.

Berkovic spent the last few months of the season warming the bench at Blackburn on a loan deal, while, with a little more application he could have been part of the seemingly never-ending party Celtic has enjoyed since the league was clinched in early April.

Berkovic, though, may have sealed his fate as early as July when he told reporters that he had no intention of changing his laconic style merely to suit O'Neill.

He spoke the day before the second game of Celtic's pre-season tour in Copenhagen. The words were not what Martin wanted to hear.

Berkovic said: "The new manager cannot bring anything to my game. I won't change it and I don't need to prove anything.

"I have shown people what I can do. If they like it, fine. If they don't, that's fine as well.

"I go out to do my best and I play the game the way I play it.

"Nobody expects me to play like Johan Mjallby and nobody expects Johan Mjallby to play like me.

"I always work hard but I don't tackle much because that's not my game.

"If I make tackles and don't do it properly, I could be injured and being out for two months would not help the team."

Berkovic didn't have to worry about that for too long. O'Neill could afford the luxury of only one fantasy player in his line-up, and as Lubo Moravcik was prepared to graft as well as craft openings, he got the nod.

Berkovic sat on the bench and in the stand for months before being shipped out to Ewood Park and a reunion with his former manager Graeme Souness.

It is fair to say his presence has not been missed by the men he left behind.

NINE

HAD Bible John ever been brought to book chances are Martin O'Neill would have been spotted in the public gallery of Glasgow High Court following every step of the trial.

The Celtic manager would claim to be more interested in the likes of Ally McCoist than Ally McBeal. But only just.

O'Neill's love of football holds sway over the other great interest in his life - the law - but it's a close run thing.

He would have become a barrister had his ability with a ball at his feet not plucked him from Queen's University, Belfast, in 1972 and sent him on a footballing adventure that shows no sign of coming to an end 29 years on.

O'Neill's fascination with the law, and with high profile murder cases in particular, did not diminish with his withdrawal from his studies.

Mention the name James Hanratty in his company, for instance, and you might just see the Irishman snap to attention.

The case of Hanratty, the last convincted British killer to be hanged back in 1961, has intrigued O'Neill since he was a teenager in his hometown of Kilrea.

In fact, the fate of the man who was known as the A62 murderer – but whose innocence was protested long after his death by his family and friends – sparked Martin's initial interest in the legal system and drove him towards his degree course.

The move to Nottingham did nothing to deflect his enthusiasm for the legal process and away from training and playing he spent hours poring over law books and case studies.

So much so, that he queued to see the trial of Yorkshire Ripper Peter Sutcliffe and has made a point of visiting the cell in which JFK assassin Lee Harvey Oswald spent his last night before gunned down by Jack Ruby.

O'Neill also followed avidly from the public gallery, the Black Panther trial, in which Donald Neilson was convicted and the Celtic manager admitted: "I have a big interest in crime and criminology.

"As a kid I was interested in the case of James Hanratty and that continued into my university days where the part of of my law course that interested me most was criminology.

"For the Ripper trial, I queued overnight with my heavily pregnant wife. We lined up for the 9am start and were the last two to be let in. There must have been 200 people behind us in the queue.

"I did the same at Oxford when Neilson was on the witness stand at the Crown Court. Hearing him give evidence was very harrowing, but I do find it interesting.

"My daughters think I'm a bit weird but I don't think so. It has to be a celebrated case or one in which there is an element of doubt."

During his time at Leicester City, O'Neill befriended Scottish journalist Bill Anderson and their professional relationship – Anderson the sports reporter covering Leicester City – led to a personal friendship and one of their shared interests away from football is a fixation with high profile criminal cases.

"Martin doesn't have much time away from football but he loves murder trials and the JFK case is one that has fascinated him for years," says Anderson.

"He took Leicester on an end of season trip to Florida one year and while there he took a detour to Dallas to witness the scene of the shooting.

"He got into a cab to go to Lee Harvey Oswald's house but the taxi driver didn't know where it was. But Martin did – he had read so much about the case that he was able to give a Dallas cabbie directions.

"There was also an office across from the book depository, which at time of the assassination had a window open and in a few xposes it had been speculated that shots actually came from there.

"He went to the building and asked if he could have a look around. He ended up walking into some guy's office and the guy just stood up and walked out, leaving him to examine the view from the window.

"He also went to the county jail where Oswald was shot. It's all changed now but he saw this policeman and mentioned he was interested in the case.

"The policeman told him that they still had the orginal cells, so he persuaded the guy to allow him to into the cell where Oswald was held.

"He loved getting that close to a fascinating piece of history.

"The workings of the criminal mind obviously interests him. He was studying to be a lawyer, so I suppose that is not too surprising."

O'Neill chose football, but it hasn't stopped him making a case for the defence ever since. Anyone who has tried to get past Johan Mjallby, Joos Valgaeren and Ramon Vega would testify to that.

TEN

JIMMY NICHOLL shares more than his nationality with Martin O'Neill.

He, too, embraces the theory that there is no need to use one word in a sentence when ten or eleven will do.

Ask the current Dunfermline assistant manager, who shared the international football stage with O'Neill for the decade between 1976 and 1986, to provide an insight into the man's life with Northern Ireland and the words tumble out so quickly they are in danger of knocking each other over in the rush to escape.

Nicholl the right back played behind O'Neill the right midfielder in two World Cups. They were part of the team whose name is written indelibly in the pages of the competition's history books for pulling off the shock of the 1982 competition when they beat hosts Spain in their own hostile back yard.

O'Neill wore the captain's armband that marvellous night in Valencia and 19 years on the memory of the victory still brings a smile to Nicholl's face.

So, too, does the recollection of international life with O'Neill. The picture he paints is a colourful one and the canvas he uses is broad.

O'Neill, he contends, was never your archetypal footballer. For instance, while most players spent their free time in the bookies, Martin WAS a bookie.

"And not just among the lads either," says Nicholl. "This wasn't a two-bit operation with him setting himself up to take other players' bets.

"He was always on the phone talking to a couple of his brothers, who seemed to run the bookies' business for him.

"We'd come in from training to find Martin lying on the treatment table with a phone glued to his ear telling one brother to lay off this bet and another brother to lay off that one.

"He was also reading the Sporting Life and any other betting paper he could get his hands on. I don't think he was a massive gambler himself - he was too smart for that."

According to Nicholl, and those who know O'Neill won't be surprised to read this, Martin was the man at the centre of most of the socialising that went on with the Northern Ireland squad even if he wasn't a big drinker.

Nicholl added: "We'd turn up for international duty on the Sunday and that was always the night we were allowed a few beers.

"We all got on brilliantly and the chat would be flowing. Martin would be at the centre of it, telling stories about Brian Clough and what he'd been up to.

"He was a master story teller but he'd go on and on and on.

"He didn't drink much – just a couple of lagers – but I'm afraid some of the boys had to drink a wee bit more than that just to help them sleep. Otherwise Martin would have kept us awake all night."

O'Neill may have been the joker of the pack but come kick off time, the man who would become Celtic manager was deadly serious.

Nicholl added: "As I recall, he preferred a wee rub on the treatment table to training on a Monday and Tuesday but you should have seen him on the day of the game.

"That's when he came alive and I suspect Martin is exactly the same today. The thought of the match galvanises him and the people around him respond to him. I came into the international set-up a few years after him but he was still one of the youngest in the squad. It didn't stop him going around geeing up the older guys like Pat Jennings, Bryan Hamilton and Pat Rice.

"He absolutely lived for the 90 minutes and on the park he had the ability to lift your confidence all the time. Even if I played an average pass, he'd be ruffling my hair and saying: 'Jimmy, that was brilliant.'

"His enthusiasm was totally infectious and it rubbed off on anyone who was playing in the same team as him. We had a fantastic team spirit and he was a prime factor in that."

The Northern Ireland that Nicholl and O'Neill represented in the 70s and 80s was, of course, riven by religious divide.

The Troubles were at their height but although the national team was populated by both Protestant and Catholic players, Nicholl insists that no friction existed within the confines of the squad.

He joked: "The only rule we had was that the Catholics all roomed together – that's why I never shared a room with Martin!

"No, it was obviously a serious situation at times and before we would gather for games we'd get a letter telling us where we'd be staying.

"On more than one occasion that would be followed by a phone call from the Irish Football Association informing us to go to a different hotel because the original one had been bombed.

"But the players in the squad never bickered about religion and the time, I honestly don't remember our fans ever having a go at any of our Catholic players."

The fact that O'Neill, a Catholic, went onto become his country's captain underlined the togetherness within the squad and the Celtic manager went on to win 64 caps before a serious knee injury finished his career in 1984.

By then his thoughts were turning to coaching and although it took O'Neill until 1987 to land his first managerial job at non-league Grantham Town, Nicholl had no doubt he would become a success.

He added: "Put it this way – Martin would have been a success at whatever he turned his mind to. He is a very clever man and he has the ability to talk his way into anything.

"But football is his great love and it was inevitable that he would be a success.

"He gave up a career in law for it, but you know he'd have been a great lawyer as well.

"He used to come in and tell us that he'd be sitting through court cases - I think he spent every day at the Peter Sutcliffe trial in the early 80s.

"To some people that might seem odd, but not to me. He was interested in the law, so it seemed to make sense.

"If he had been sitting behind a bush birdwatching for nine hours a day, I'd have thought that odd – but not a former law student watching criminal trials.

"What I wondered, though, was how he find the time to do it.

"But somehow Martin always managed."

Twenty years on, he's still managing. And managing very nicely.

O'Neill played 64 times for Northern Ireland but also took part in a unique match that became part of Irish footballing folklore in 1973.

The young Nottingham Forest player was chosen to turn out for an all-Ireland team that took on the then-world champions Brazil in Dublin.

The match caused a political storm at a time when The Troubles in the north were taking hold, but 34,000 watched the unified team lose by only 4-3 to a Brazilian team that contained players of the calibre of Jairzinho, Rivelino and Clodoaldo.

One of the players involved that day, Wolves' Northern Ireland striker Derek Dougan, said: "You have to understand half of this Brazil team had been part of the greatest side ever to play the game in 1970. What makes it special is that I know fans from both sides of the community in the North travelled down to get a glimpse of the best of the Irish taking them on."

Former Celtic coach Mick Martin was on Manchester United's books at the time and play against the South Americans.

He recalled: "Like all great sport, this was about having fun. The players from Northern Ireland and the Republic knew each other to play against in England and, for us, sport and politics could never mix.

"We laughed and joked in the dressing room beforehand and afterwards, just like we did when playing with the Republic. At the end of the day, we were just footballers."

ELEVEN

IF Hollywood ever gets round to making a movie about the life and times of Martin O'Neill and John Robertson, they'd have to wheel out Jack Lemmon and Walter Matthau to play the lead roles.

After all, they've already rehearsed for the part in The Odd Couple.

Brian Clough accepts that O'Neill and Robbo are complete opposites and always were. And while he had to work hard at liking Martin in the early days, he took an instant shine to the rogue that was Robbo.

"I know Martin goes on about Robbo being my favourite son and that I didn't care much for him. He was possibly right," Clough smiles.

" You couldn't help like Robbo, even if he was a tramp. I used to go through the main door of the club in the mornings, but Robbo would stand at the door of our Jubilee social club just along the road having his last fag before coming in for training.

" I put up with it for a while then finally told him to get his act together. He just changed tactics. He would stand at the corner, peering round to see when my car coming then stub the fag out.

"He didn't like to shave, he's not exactly like Robert Redford and he had the unfortunate build on him that defied anyone guessing that he was an athlete.

"He always had suede shoes that were always covered in chip fat. I used to say the binmen would refuse to take them away if he put them out.

"But for all that, and for the fact that he was a lazy sod, Robbo could play.

"Very few people realise just how good a player Robbo was. He was fat and he was short, but give him the ball at his feet and an inch to cross it and he would put it into the danger area.

"He wouldn't run back when we didn't have the ball. I kept telling him: 'Robbo, the halfway line doesn't move towards you - you have to move towards it when we don't have the ball.

"But he was brilliant. I just said to the players: 'When you are in trouble, give the ball to Robbo. You know where he'll be because the lazy bugger never bloody moves.'"

The friendship between Robertson and O'Neill had been struck before Clough arrived in 1974.

The former Forest manager added: "He and Martin were complete opposites but they were great pals.

"For instance, Martin wasn't much of a drinker. He was a half of lager man. John would have a little bit more. Just about enough to have sunk the Titanic.

"Even before I got to the club they were mates. They came into the side together, they roomed together and both learned their trades together.

"They gelled on the field because they were opposites style-wise. Robertson didn't have to be told to play the ball, it came automatically, while Martin would want to touch it five times.

"When I brought all these so called stars in, those two would give them stick by saying: 'We built this club before you came.'

"They hadn't, of course, but I liked my players to have a bit of cheek and they had that."

O'Neill is not the type to ask anyone for advice too often but shortly after entering management for the first time, he picked up the phone and asked Clough how to go about appointing an assistant.

Clough recalled: "I remember telling him to make sure the guy he chose was a pal.

"When you are a manager, the buck stops with you. It's not the assistant manager who gets stick from the fans and the Press when things aren't going right - it's you.

"So, if you are going to get the stick you might as well get it for the decisions you make – not for decisions that some smart-arsed assistant might be making.

"That's why I said he should appoint a pal. Someone he could talk to openly and someone he could trust, but ultimately someone who appreciated that the manager is the guy who has to make the big decisions.

"He chose Robertson and it wasn't a real surprise because they were always close.

"John has a great football brain, he had to have to play the way he did, but he is also really good company and if Martin if feeling under pressure he will be a great help to him.

"I had a great partnership witb Peter Taylor for years and one of the reasons was that he understood that when it came to making the big decisions, I was the one who made them.

"I'm sure John feels the same about his partnership with Martin."

Their partnership has lasted longer than most Hollywood marriages - from Grantham to Shepsted, like a young couple starting out in a room and kitchen, to the terraced house of Wycombe, the semi detached villa at Leicester and finally to the mansion that looms over all it surrounds in the east end of Glasgow.

The relationship broke up during O'Neill's six-month spell at Norwich, when Robertson's family commitments meant that he was unable to work full-time in football.

Significantly, O'Neill found the job his most difficult in football and after a series of run-ins with chairman Robert Chase finally walked out to take the Leicester job and persuade Robertson to rejoin him.

Had Robertson been at his side at Carrow Road, the Irishman might have coped better with the frustration he felt at being unable to prise money from Chase to fund his team strengthening plans.

Robertson was back at his side at Filbert Street and has rarely left it since. Only the short period between O'Neill joining Celtic and his new employers sorting out compensation with Leicester for Robertson and his other loyal lieutenant Steve Walford saw them apart again.

Walford is the man O'Neill entrusts to put his ideas across to the players on the training ground. Robertson is more of a sounding board on which he bounces those ideas before sending Walford out to put them into practice.

As engaging and approachable as he is, however, anyone who thinks that Robertson is little more than a 'social convener' – a tag affixed to Terry McDermott during Kenny Dalglish and John

Barnes' stint at Celtic – would be way off the mark.

The former Scotland winger recently tried to explain the mix that has brought them so much success.

"He trusts me," he said. "He thinks I know a bit and I'm grateful for the chances he's given me.

"The important things are what people don't see, when you are sitting in the office every day discussing things.

"Martin will say: 'What do you think? ' and knows I'll give an honest opinion. Whether he takes it on board is his ultimate responsibility. He's the boss."

Robertson took a shine to O'Neill from the day the young Irish kid walked through the gates of Nottingham Forest's City Ground for the first time back in the early 70s.

They were, he concedes, different but they shared a love of the game and a desire to succeed in it – even if the picture Brian Clough paints of Robertson is one of a talented toe-rag.

Robbo added: "What I can about that – images stick don't they.

"Clough liked me. I never got too much of a bollocking and shrugged it off when I did. Martin, by nature, was more likely to answer back."

As for comparing O'Neill and Clough, Robertson has this to say: "Brian had a kind heart yet he could be very brash and harsh while Martin's more consistent in how he treats people.

"They are completely different personalities but they've got the same gift in different ways.

"Their gift is that they make players want to work hard for them. They've got something special - charisma is the only word that comes close to describing it - and when they speak, people listen.

"Martin is not one to spend a whole day coaching, but what's a coach? If someone tells you something that makes sense, that's good coaching. Whether it happens on the training pitch or it's a word in the ear in somebody's office is not important.

"With Clough, I just wanted him to praise me. He'd give me a little sign from the dug-out to say I was doing well and when I saw it my heart would swell. Martin's got the same influence on people."

It seems the Odd Couple still has long time to run.

TWELVE

GRANTHAM, Lincolnshire. The birthplace of Margaret Thatcher but every town has its cross to bear.

It has another claim to fame, though, and this is not one that divides the local population as allegiances to the Iron Lady once did.

Grantham is also the place that gave birth to Martin O'Neill's managerial career and there is universal pride in that fact from the town's footballing fraternity.

In the summer of 1987, three years after a cruciate knee ligament injury ended his playing career at 32, O'Neill took his first faltering steps on a journey that was to lead from

London Road, Grantham, to London Road, Glasgow.

Those who saw him take them were convinced from almost the beginning that the Irishman had a talent that set him apart from his peers.

Grantham Town Supporters Club chairman Graham Cowell certainly believed. The part-time Lincolnshire club might have been playing in front of only 300 people at the time but the bundle of nervous energy bouncing around the touchline demanded that his players gave him everything and made him a target of terracing taunts from opposite supporters.

O'Neill took it in his stride until the day Grantham visited Haylesowen Town – and O'Neill ended up climbing a wire fence to try to get at his tormentors.

Cowell will never forget the day the Celtic manager almost went over the top – literally.

He said: "You've seen it all the way through his career – he is passionate about football and about HIS football teams.

"He would always talk to people about football and sometimes he would agree with them and sometimes disagree.

"That afternoon at Haylesowen was incredible. He had been getting grief from their supporters all game and they've got fencing up behind the dug-outs at their ground.

"At the end of the match, he ran at the fence and started clambering up it. He was hanging off it giving someone the finger.

"I think we lost the game but should have won it and Martin was very frustrated.

"Their fans were going mental but Martin was more interested in getting his point across than in caring about what they thought of him.

"It just summed up how passionate he was about the game and obviously he still is. We loved him for it."

O'Neill's introduction to management was a painful one, however. The Grantham boss lost his first game in charge in deepest, darkest South Wales.

Cowell continued: "When Martin was appointed he had a commitment to coach in America, but he arrived back in Britain the day we were due to play Merthyr Tydfil.

"He was driven straight from the airport to the game in Wales and we lost 3-0. It could hardly have been described as the ideal start in the most glamorous surroundings, but he was off and running after that."

O'Neill might have been part-time but having waited so long for a managerial opening, it is perhaps not surprising that he threw his heart and soul into the job.

Shortly before Grantham came calling he thought he had finally cracked it with Bradford City.

O'Neill later said: "I did well. Of the eight candidates, I was the only one invited back for a second interview. But they went for Terry Dolan, who'd done well as caretaker manager. Only an Irishman, I suppose, could be the last one left on the shortlist and still not get the job."

Bradford's loss was Grantham's gain – and Tony Balfe's in particular.

Financial advisor Balfe had just taken over as chairman of the Beazer Homes League club – these days they play in the Dr Marten's League – and was on the lookout for a new manager.

These days Balfe's association with the club is as a supporter but it is with pride that he admits he is the man who gave Martin O'Neill the chance to become a football manager.

Even if he did only pay him £60 a week.

Balfe said: "When I took over the club, I'd heard that Martin was looking to get into management.

"Obviously, we are just up the road from Nottingham, so we knew all about his pedigree.

"I contacted him, we met in a pub and over a couple of drinks and a chat we agreed that he would become our new manager.

"Even then, he had definite ideas about what he wanted. For instance, he insisted that he should be allowed to sit in on board meetings because he wanted to know everything about running the club.

"We had debts of £30,000 at the time and giving him an adequate budget was difficult.

"That didn't deter him though – he simply threw himself into fund-raising activities and he managed to persuade some of his former Nottingham Forest team-mates like Kenny Burns and John Robertson to play for us, which was exciting for our supporters.

"We just missed out on promotion in the first season and finished fifth in the second season. After that, Martin came to us looking for finance to help us take the next step, but we simply couldn't come up with it.

"He had the knack of making players produce their very best and in the two seasons he was with us, I think he actually only spent mooney on one signing and that was for all of £500.

"He came from a big family and he always understood the value of spending carefully and wisely. That is something he continued to this day.

"But in the end, we simply could not match his ambition. He wanted to take us further but we couldn't make any money available to him and we lost him to another non-league club, Shepstone Charterhouse.

"Before long, he was at Wycombe Wanderers in the conference, and of course that is when things really started to take off for Martin.

"He's come a long way since those days. I don't know what he'll be on at Celtic, but we could only afford £60 a week.

"He supplemented his income by working with the Save and Prosper insurance firm, where I think he did some promotional work for them.

"But he spent most of his time with us and it is good to know he has not forgotten his roots.

"He called me a couple of years ago from a hotel in London, where he had Leicester City resting up before playing in the League Cup Final.

"We had a great old chat about the club and about the times we spent together.

"Martin was about to take his team into one of the most important games of his career but he was chatting away to me as if he had nothing better to do on a Sunday afternoon.

"That kind of sums up the fella."

Grantham Town's stadium at the time, the London Road Ground, is now a Safeway. But Martin O'Neill no longer has to scrape in the bargain basement bins.

That doesn't mean he has forgotten the days when he did.

THIRTEEN

HAD the part-time Vauxhall Conference team been named Aimless Wanderers rather than Wycombe Wanderers nobody would have batted an eyelid.

This, you see, was a club drifting in the bottom half of the tier which operates below the senior leagues in England and who didn't have any particular desire to be anywhere else.

Then Martin O'Neill arrived at the start of 1990 and gave the tiny Buckinghamshire team a sense of direction. Suddenly the wandering around in the dark stopped and Wycombe began moving, purposefully, in an upwards direction.

They didn't stop when they got to the top of the Conference and gatecrashed their way into the English Third Division in the summer of 1993.

They simply kept winning games and within a year Wycombe were in the Second Division. That's where they remain to this day and O'Neill continues to be lionized around those parts.

Dave Carroll doesn't try to underplay O'Neill's role in the club's history. The Paisley-born midfielder holds Wycombe Wanderers' appearance record and has witnessed at first hand the rise of the club and is still a vital member of the team 14 years down the line.

He said: "To realise how far we've come, you've got understand where we were before Martin arrived. We were in the bottom half of the Conference and didn't look like going anywhere.

"We had good players but no sense of direction and needed someone to get the best out of us.

"We were playing at Loakes Park, which was a bit run-down, but within six months we had moved to our current stadium Adams Park.

"Martin demanded that we worked hard – he drummed into us that we would only get out of the game what we put in.

"I remember his first day like yesterday. I arrived late and walked in to see him standing there. He said nothing but gave me a dirty look.

"We only trained two nights a week in those days and on the second night I was late as well. Again, he didn't say anything but when the team was picked for the Saturday I was dropped.

"I soon got the message. He commanded respect immediately and his theme was that we were better than other teams, and if we put in the effort, our ability would come through.

"Looking at the way he's worked at Leicester and at Celtic, I would say that he hasn't changed that philosphy.

"He has better players at his disposal now but he still insists they work their socks off – and players want to do it for him."

Even Jason Cousins. And even after what O'Neill did to him when he was sent off for the second game in a row at Wycombe.

Cousins recalled: "About eight years ago I was sent off two games in succession and the second one was for a horror tackle on David Moss, who was at Doncaster at the time.

"I was in the shower with soap in my eyes when Martin came in, grabbed me and threw me outside into the corridor. I was just standing there stark naked."

O'Neill was angry enough to strip Cousins, nicknamed Psycho, of the captaincy and banned him from the ground for a week.

But the long-serving Wycombe player bounced back and is still a vital member of their squad long after O'Neill turned the club's fortunes around.

O'Neill admits he had big plans for Wycombe from the moment he walked through the gates of Loakes Park. And he achieved all of them.

Shortly after leaving Wycombe, the Celtic manager said: "I don't care who you are, what you do, how you go about life – people do dream.

"It's what keeps them hanging on sometimes, gives them an

incentive and becomes the ultimate driving force.

"Me? I've always done it. Still do and don't want to stop. You don't want to put a brake on something you believe in.

"When I was manager of Grantham Town, I dreamed of getting them out of the Beazer Homes League and into the Vauxhall Conference.

"Then when I managed Wycombe, I would close my eyes and imagine taking them into the Football League.

"Flights of fancy sustained me. Nothing wrong with that and some of them came true."

O'Neill recently invited Carroll, Cousins and several long – serving Wycombe players and staff to Parkhead for the clash with Rangers that ended in a 1-0 victory for Celtic.

Carroll added: "It was a fantastic day and he made sure we were treated superbly.

"He came in for a chat an hour before kick-off and we were saying to him: 'Martin, shouldn't you be in the dressing room?'.

"But he said everything was under control and he wanted to make sure we were being looked after. He hadn't changed a bit and I don't think he ever will.

Cousins said: "Martin made a beeline for us and we were all in his office having a chat about 45 minutes before kick off. We said that he was looking very relaxed before such a big game but he admitted to us: 'I am absolutely s****** myself."

Wycombe clearly appealed to O'Neill and his family. They retained their family home on the outskirts of the town when they moved to Norwich and Leicester.

And although they are settled into their family home in Edinburgh these days, the house in Wycombe continues to waiting for the day the O'Neills head back south.

Legions of Celtic fans hope the O'Neill residence lies empty for quite some time to come.

DREAMING OF GLORY ... Martin loved playing football in the back garden of his council house home in Kilrea, County Derry

TOP TEAM ... Martin (front with cup) and St Columb's gaelic football side

SUITS YOU ... the O'Neill brothers attend a family wedding

CUP HEROES ... Martin (back right) won the 1971 Irish Cup with Distillery

DOUBLE ACT ... Distillery boss Jimmy McAlinden congratulates Martin after O'Neill's two goals sealed a 3-1 win over Derry City in the Irish Cup final

EUR THE MEN ... Martin and friend Raymond White (back left)
prepare to board Distillery's flight to Barcelona for their big European tie

BEST BUDDIES ... Martin is still friendly with old pal Raymond White

MENTOR ... Brian Clough and Martin together during their days at Forest

KID CLASS ... O'Neill in his early days at Nottingham Forest

MAESTRO ... Martin takes control against Hamburg in the 1980
European Cup final – Nottingham Forest beat the Germans 1-0

PARTY TIME ... Forest players celebrate after their historic win over Hamburg

WHO'S THE BOSS ... O'Neill challenges Arsenal's Liam Brady – who also
went on to manage Celtic, but without the same success as Martin

WEMBLEY WAY ... against Southampton in the 1979 League Cup Final

RE-UNITED ... Brian Clough and Martin are still friends after their Forest years

BATTLER ... Martin in action for Norwich – a club he would later manage

COUNTY ME IN ... Martin starred for Notts County before he retired

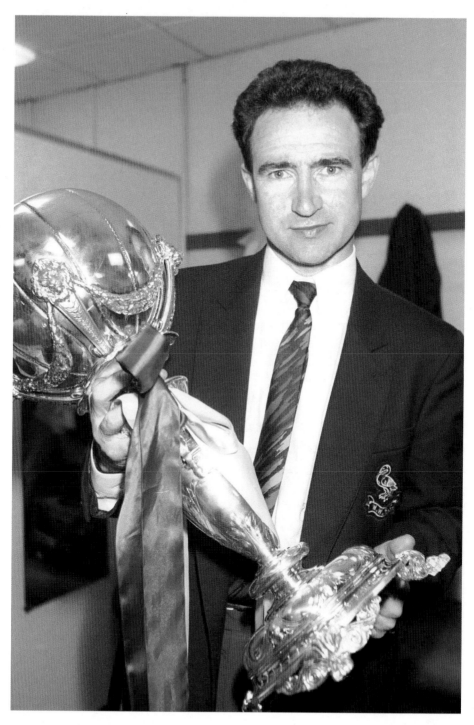

EARLY GLORY ... Martin lifted the FA Challenge trophy as Wycombe boss

MATT'S THE WAY TO DO IT ... Martin celebrates Leicester's
Worthington Cup win in 2000 with Filbert Street captain Matt Elliot

PARADISE FOUND ... O'Neill is paraded as Celtic's new manager

WINNING START ... goalscorers Chris Sutton and Henrik Larsson
celebrate an opening day league win over Dundee United at Tannadice

JOY OF SIX ... Sutton shows his delight after scoring in Celtic's 6-2 Old Firm win

STAN THE MAN ... Petrov celebrates his strike in the 6-2 demolition derby

JUMPING FOR JOY ... Martin can't hide his delight during the 6-2 triumph over Rangers – his first Old Firm derby as Celtic manager

ON THE SHOULDER OF A GIANT ... Martin O'Neill is determined
to follow legendary Celtic boss Jock Stein into the history books

LENNON AID ... Neil arrived in December to help Celtic's title quest

HAT-TRICK HERO ... Henrik's third against Killie seals the CIS Cup win

LEAGUE OF THEIR OWN ... Tommy Johnson's goal clinched the title in
a hard-fought 1-0 victory over St Mirren in April at Celtic Park

HERO ... Martin takes the applause of the fans after Celtic's championship win

THE TALISMEN ... O'Neill and Larsson have led Celtic to glory this season

SILVER STREAK ... Martin and Paul Lambert with the League trophy

CUP OF CHEER ... McNamara celebrates his opening goal in the Cup final

HAIL THE HEROES ... the team salute the fans outside Celtic Park after
beating Hibs 3-0 to lift the Scottish Cup and complete a glorious treble

CAPTAIN MARVELS ... Paul Lambert and Tom Boyd savour lifting the Cup

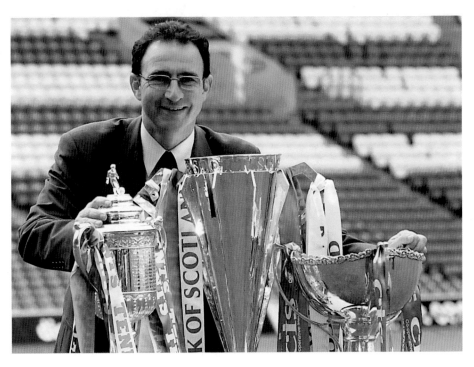

SILVER SERVICE ... Martin shows off the fruits of a successful season

THE POWER AND THE GLORY ... Martin with the Scottish Cup

FOURTEEN

LEICESTER CITY fans laughed when they learned Celtic had made a move to lure Martin O'Neill from Filbert Street.

After all, they reckoned, why would their manager leave one of the best championships in the world for a two-bit league set-up in Scotland?

But they didn't figure on the emotional pull Celtic were able to exert on the Irishman and when the penny finally dropped that O'Neill was leaving last June, the news was treated like a death in the family.

The wailing and wringing of hands couldn't have been any more different from five years earlier when the Filbert Street support would have been wringing his neck if they'd got the chance.

O'Neill had come to Leicester from Norwich at Christmas 1995 with a reputation as being one of the best up and coming managers in the game. But an opening record of no wins from ten matches had the fans demanding that he be shown the door.

The situation came to a head in a match against Sheffield United when O'Neill confronted hundreds of fans who had stayed behind to stage a demonstration at the end of a 3-1 defeat.

The supporters appreciated the manager's bottle and from that day on the relationship improved dramatically, as did the results.

Leicester went on to make the First Division play-offs and beat Crystal Palace at Wembley to reach the promised land of the Premiership.

The combative part of O'Neill's nature, however, never allowed him to forget that the people who came to idolise him had at one point shunned him.

The man who scored the goal that took Leicester into the big time, Steve Claridge, remembers clearly that O'Neill was not one to forgive and forget too easily.

Claridge said: "Martin's not the sort of man to do that too easily. He reminded the supporters of that fact many times and he was perfectly entitled to do so.

"Too many people are far too quick to judge in this game and that was the case when Martin first joined Leicester.

"Things got so bad after one home game against Sheffield United we had to get a police escort out of the back entrance of the club because there was a mass demonstration.

"But that was the turning point for us. After that we started winning games, then got to the play-offs and won them.

"He didn't get off to the best of starts but despite not getting a victory for the first few months, the indications were always that he would get on fine because he is one of the few managers who can actually change things around quickly and make them work."

While Leicester's players scuttled out of Filbert Street by the tradesman's door on the day they lost to Sheffield United, O'Neill didn't.

He faced the mob and gained a respect that grew and grew until the day he left for Celtic and beyond.

Leicester City Supporters Club chairman Cliff Ginetta explained the events of the day Sheffield United came calling.

He said: "The first 10 games weren't very good and it climaxed with a game against Sheffield United at Filbert Street, when there was a big demonstration from the Kop end of the ground.

"Martin took it to heart. He thought the fans were just having a go at him but it was directed at the Board as well. They felt that more money should be made available.

"Martin had three new players in that day, Neil Lennon, Muzzy Izzet and Julian Watts – none of them was a big money signing and the crowd wasn't happy.

"He took some stick. The minority started it and it built up and got a bit of out hand.

"But he won the respect of the fans that day because he fronted us up and didn't hide. He was shouting at us: 'Give me time, I've only been here a couple of months.'

"The police would not let him come out and stand in front of the Kop end. They were worried that there were so many people there that things could get out of hand.

"But Martin insisted that they took some people out of the Kop and took them to the track outside the tunnel area where Martin was waiting.

"He told us that he would get it right if he was given the chance to do the job right and he asked us to go back to the fans and tell them to judge him in a little while.

"After that we had quite a good run and we realised that although Lennon and Izzet weren't big names at the time, they were terrific players.

"We won a few games and made the play-offs, and of course we beat Crystal Palace at Wembley to win promotion."

O'Neill had been forgiven for his dreadful start. But he forgotten.

Ginetta added: "Martin took it personally and he never let us forget it. He always brought it up during the good times.

"He was always saying that he knew that a few bad results would have his job under threat again like it was in the early days.

"Some of it might have been said tongue in cheek but there was always an edge behind the humour.

"He was getting stick in the local paper and when he read something he didn't like in the letters page, he wrote letters back to the people and he even phoned a few of them up.

"He kept a close ear on radio phone-ins as well. He pulled me up a couple of times for things I'd said in the papers and I wasn't even criticising him. But he'd say he didn't the like the tone of the comments.

"He collared me at the training ground one day and another time at a social function and had a few moans about the fans.

"He'd say: "What the hell is up with you lot – what do you expect from me?'

"But after the initial period he won over the fans and when he left here he was a total God."

Leicester, the corner shop competing against the hypermarkets of Manchester United, Chelsea and Arsenal, were never out of the top 10 in England under O'Neill.

That kind of miracle working on a weekly basis was bound to attract attention from elsewhere and although O'Neill had been approached by the likes of Leeds and Everton, he remained at

Filbert Street until Celtic made their move.

Ginetta said: "We always hoped against hope that he wouldn't go but we knew it would be inevitable. He nearly went to Leeds and Everton and we feared that perhaps we weren't big enough.

"But nobody down here thought that he would go to Celtic.

"No disrespect, but we thought the Scottish League would not offer him enough of a challenge.

"We felt that if he left it would be to a Liverpool or, eventually, Manchester United. Most people still feel that he will eventually end up at Old Trafford.

"But the Leicester fans always look for the Celtic result on a Saturday and a cheer goes up in our clubhouse when they've won, which is most weeks.

"The loyalty towards him has waned a little, because we feel he poached Lennon, who was a very popular player here.

"That maybe ended the love affair a little bit, but to Leicester fans he was the best manager we've ever hard and nobody can take that away from him."

The love affair, if that's what it was, seems to have been one-sided, though. The pain of the early days continued to nag at O'Neill and had he taken the course of action he wanted to on play-off day at Wembley, the relationship might have been dashed forever.

A friend of O'Neill said: "He didn't ever forget the fact the Leicester fans gave him a hard time initially. He had this thing in the back of his mind that when they got to Wembley for the First Division play-off, if they won he was going to turn to the supporters and give them the V-sign.

"In the end he didn't do that – he consoled himself by sticking his tongue out at them when he lifted the trophy at Wembley."

FIFTEEN

HE might come across as a happy-go-lucky sort of guy but beneath the welcoming exterior lies a completely different animal.

Strip away the affability, the story for every occasion and the compulsion to wander off at so many tangents that he might have been a maths teacher in a previous life, and you find a hard-nosed individual who usually gets exactly what he wants.

Martin O'Neill demands total control of team affairs and will settle for nothing less. It's his way or the highway as former Norwich City chairman Robert Chase found to his cost at the tail end of 1995.

Former Leicester City chief executive Barry Pierpoint also learned the hard way that you cross the Irishman at your peril.

Chase paid the price for failing to keep the promises that were made to O'Neill when he was offered the Norwich job in June '95.

He had driven Wycombe Wanderers from the wilderness of the Vauxhall Conference to the English Second Division in five years – a turbo-charged journey in such a short time.

Carrow Road chairman Chase targetted Martin as the man who could lead his East Anglian club back to the Premiership and tempted him with the promise of £5m-£6m to spend on strengthening the squad.

O'Neill was far too ambitious to spend too long thinking about it and smart enough to realise that it was impossible to take Wycombe any further – six years on they still haven't been able to escape the league he left them in, although they did reach this season's FA Cup semi final.

The Irishman jumped at the move to the Norfolk club but when he went knocking on the chairman's door for the promised transfer kitty, he found it locked and bolted from the inside.

Chase finally emerged to hand over a paltry £650,000 which secured the signature of former Rangers and Scotland striker Robert Fleck but in spite of repeated attempts to persuade the chairman to part with more cash, O'Neill's pleas fell on deaf ears.

Matters finally came to a head in November when the plug was pulled on a deal that would have taken former Aberdeen striker Dean Windass, at Hull at the time, to Norwich.

O'Neill had agreed a £750,000 with the Humberside club but two months after the move had been given the thumbs up, Chase still hadn't shown O'Neill the money to finalise the deal.

Finally, Hull ran out of patience. They weren't alone. O'Neill was at the end of his tether and no longer had the desire to work with his chairman.

A month later he walked out – and strode into a storm. On the day he quit, Norwich were scheduled to play managerless Leicester City and O'Neill became their boss just five days later.

Allegations that a deal had been struck with O'Neill before he quit Norwich have always been vehemently denied but what is clear is the fact that the Filbert Street club took full advantage of Martin disillusionment with Chase.

At the time, Leicester were a mid-table First Division club like Norwich and the move was seen as a sideways rather than upward step.

Under his stewardship, however, they reached the play-offs and were promoted to the Premiership in his first season and before leaving for Celtic, O'Neill guided the Midlands club to top 10 finishes in each of its five seasons in the big time.

He rarely talks about his time at Carrow Road but let slip his true feelings on one occasion by stating: "Norwich would be in the Premiership if I had stayed. It might sound big-headed but I know I would have got them promotion.

"I had too many differences of opinion with the chairman about the best way to run the club. Remarkably, I thought I could do it better than him in football terms."

The move to Filbert Street wasn't always a stroll in the sunshine either. Particularly when the club appointed Barrie Pierpoint as chief executive in 1998 and he immediately engineered moves to run the football side of the business by five-man committee, thus diluting the power O'Neill insisted was his right as team manager.

O'Neill wasn't consulted about the move and learned about it late one night when he was flicking through Teletext. Not unnaturally, he went ballistic.

Their relationship was fraught from day one – after querying a mobile phone bill on one occasion, Pierpoint later found all of O'Neill's backroom staff's mobiles in a bin liner which had been dumped on his desk.

Attached was a note and for a man who is known to love words it was cuttingly abrupt, reading: "Not happy – Martin." No phone bills were ever again queried.

O'Neill fought the five-man committee project, making it a resignation issue, and he won. He also insisted when Pierpoint was offered his next contract, he would have no part in the team affairs.

Pierpoint admitted at the time: "When I signed my contract, Martin insisted on a clause that I wouldn't get involved in team matters. I agreed, which demonstrated my commitment to him."

But the rift between the pair was never healed and a year later the gap widened to a gulf and Pierpoint was finally forced out the door.

A Boardroom battle for control of the club found two factions – one led by Pierpoint and three cohorts – vying for power with Leicester City plc chairman Sir Rodney Walker and club chairman John Elsom.

O'Neill very publicly backed the Walker-Elsom partnership and hinted not very subtly that if the shareholders sided with Pierpoint he would walk away.

That led to uproar among the rank and file supporters who held demonstrations and attended matches holding 'Don't Go Martin' placards.

At the EGM to decide the club's fate, the O'Neill endorsed partnership won a landslide victory and Pierpoint's group, known as the Gang of Four, were forced out.

Pierpoint knew the O'Neill influence had killed off his chances. With more than a trace of bitterness, he said: "I have tried for the last two or three years to work with Martin O'Neill but co-operation has not been forthcoming. I find it strange."

One of Pierpoint's partners, Philip Smith, was even more

scathing. He said: "I was always of the view that the club is bigger than the individual. But I have some doubts this is the case at Leicester.

"The manager said he supported the other side and he wouldn't work with us. The issues were presented as a choice between the manager or us.

"It would be difficult for me to state how I view Martin now."

But O'Neill knew that with Pierpoint in charge he would not have the absolute control over team matters that he craves. He sided with Elsom and Walker. The rest is history and so is Pierpoint.

Leicester City supporters' association chairman Cliff Ginetta perhaps sums it up best.

He said: "Pierpoint was a revelation in many ways but eventually he had too much power and too much ambition and didn't know what to do with it.

"I said right from the start that as soon as he took on Martin O'Neill he was dead in the water.

"It didn't need a genius to work that out but Barrie Pierpoint and his pals just couldn't see it."

SIXTEEN

TO understand the size of job Martin O'Neill accepted on June 1, 2000, one has to realise the depths to which Celtic had plummeted in the months leading up to his appointment.

Not only had the club meekly surrendered the league championship to Rangers for the 11th time in 12 years long before the previous season ended, but the manner of the defeat had cut into the soul of the support.

They finished 21 points adrift of their greatest rivals – seven whole matches worth of points – and floating among the debris of their season was the club's dignity.

It had, in effect, become a laughing stock.

The Kenny Dalglish-John Barnes partnership that had been hailed by then-chief executive Allan MacDonald as the dream team to propel Celtic to a new level of success domestically and abroad had been dismantled by the middle of February.

Barnes was the first to go, within 48 hours of Celtic's historic home defeat at the hands of a team that wasn't even in existence five years earlier.

Inverness Caledonian Thistle inflicted upon Celtic the most humiliating defeat in their proud 112-year history. They came to Parkhead as Scottish Cup sacrificial lambs but a 3-1 victory meant the ceremonial sword was swung in the direction of Barnes.

The rookie coach lost not only a football match on the night of February 8, 2000. He lost the dressing room and when that happens at a football club the manager's next port of call has to be the dole queue.

For a group of players to be brawling in the dressing room at half time of a cup tie they were losing to a lower league club says plenty about the mentality of the protagonists, but it also speaks volumes for Barnes' ability to control them.

Mark Viduka objected to being accused of not giving 100 per cent by Barnes' assistant manager Eric Black. Goalkeeper Jonathan Gould jumped in to the row in defence of the Australian, claiming that if anyone was to be accused of swinging the lead it should be Israeli internationalist Eyal Berkovic.

Barnes then told Gould to shut up and that he had not come off his goal-line all season and before anyone else could become involved in the rapidly growing rabble, Viduka had removed his boots and hurled them into the corner of the dressing room.

He refused to come out for the second half and we will never know if the striker's indiscipline would have been punished by Barnes because by the time Celtic played their next game the manager was out on his ear.

Kenny Dalglish, who had been given the title of director of football operations when he and Barnes were appointed, wasn't even in the country when the roof caved in.

Dalglish was in La Manga, in Spain, covering a youth tournament although the general perception was that he also taking advantage of some of the best golf facilities in Europe.

He was summoned back to restore order and to take the team on a temporary basis after MacDonald decided to sack Barnes but retain Dalglish.

The League Cup was won in the midst of the turmoil but it didn't even begin to paper over the cracks.

Dalglish's resentment of the media was underlined by his decision to hold all pre-match press conferences in either Baird's Bar, a Celtic diehard's pub, or on the premises of the club's supporters' association at Barrowfield.

Whether this was a move to intimidate the Press or not is irrelevant, although if he thought newspapermen would be worried about entering a pub he clearly didn't know them very well.

But whatever the motivation, the move merely accelerated the decline in the relationship between the media and the club.

Dalglish's problem was that while waging war with the Press, his team was falling further and further behind Rangers. It was open season on Celtic at a time when the club needed all the good publicity it could get.

Dalglish always insisted he didn't want the manager's job on a permanent basis and before the wretched season was over, Celtic's board of directors were looking for a new man.

For a long time, Dutch manager Guus Hiddink was courted despite fighting a losing battle in his attempt to keep Seville club Real Betis in Spain's top league.

But the club's main shareholder and powerbroker Dermot Desmond wanted one man – Martin O'Neill – and after a much publicised tug-of-love with Leicester City, he got him.

The Irishman, we have come to learn in the past year, is nothing if not meticulous. It can be assumed, therefore, that before he agreed to move, he knew exactly where Celtic were in terms of morale and public perception.

He also knew that if he could be the man to turn the club's fortunes around, he would be lionized by a support that was crying out for a hero.

He displayed a single-mindedness from the outset. O'Neill was criticised for honouring a contract with the BBC to analyse the Euro 2000 Championships in Holland and Belgium.

There was too much work to be done at Parkhead, his critics claimed, but O'Neill ignored them and went abroad. Not that his time in the Low Countries was without benefit to Celtic. During his TV work, the new Parkhead boss identified the defensive qualities of Belgian defender Joos Valgaeren and made him one of main targets.

And remember, this was even before he had seen Rafael in action.

Before setting out for Brussels and Amsterdam, O'Neill was introduced to the media and to the hundreds who had gathered in the Celtic car park on the afternoon of June 1.

He made no sweeping promises but right from the outset his words were those of a man who was determined to steer the club back onto a route to success.

O'Neill promised to do it slowly but surely. Somewhere along the line, however, he hit the accelerator.

On day one, he said: "I'm the eighth manager in nine years, so by deduction I should get at least seven-and-a-half months.

"But I'm a pragmatic person and I told the Board I won't be looking for 100 years to sort things out here. However, at the same time I realise that a manager here might need a bit of time to turn things around.

"I aim to do it as quickly as possible. I've got a three-year contract and the last thing Celtic fans will want is for me to start getting it right just when it is time for me to go out the door.

"I realise I need to make up some ground on Rangers but at the same time I realise that results and performances on the pitch will eventually determine how long I'm here.

"I'm not so blase as to think it is going to be dead easy but I'll give it my best shot. I'll love it here. It's the kind of challenge I enjoy."

Within 10 days of returning from Euro 2000, O'Neill realised just how big the challenge was going to be. He had embarked on a three-game, three-country pre-season tour with his new club – arranged before he arrived – and saw defensive deficiences that simply had to be eradicted before the real thing began at Tannadice in the SPL curtain raiser on the second last day of July.

O'Neill also saw at first hand how deeply Celtic cut into the core of communities outwith Scotland's shores. Not that he needed much affirmation of that fact, given that he had been born and brought up in a Celtic-mad family in Kilrea, Northern Ireland.

Celtic's first game under his guidance was played in Bray, a small town a few miles outside Dublin. If the town possessed any looters they would have had a field day on the afternoon of Sunday,

July 9, because it seemed that the entire population had shoehorned itself inside Bray Wanderers' tiny Carlisle Ground to see the beginning of O'Neill's reign.

The attendance was given at 6000 but they sprawled out almost onto the touchline, they climbed lamp-posts and fences, anything to catch a glimpse.

And through it all, O'Neill smiled. Normally dressed in training top and tracksuit trousers crammed deep inside football socks and trainers, the Irishman on this occasion wore a smart suit and the club tie.

He was proud and he was proud to show he was proud.

The match meant nothing in terms of the result, although Tommy Johnson who would clinch the championship with the only goal of the game against St Mirren nine months later, scored a hat-trick to give Celtic a 3-2 win.

The three pleased O'Neill, the two in the deficit column didn't. Rafael's performance left him stunned.

Celtic had forked out £5m on the young Brazilian back in

January. Dalglish and Barnes had sanctioned the transfer but neither had seen the defender play in person.

Illness and injury had restricted his appearances in the tail end of the season of disaster, but the fleeting glimpses did not fill the Celtic support with hope that their team had found a gem.

Seeing Rafael being turned inside out and corkscrewed into the ground by an unknown Irish kid called Jason Byrne didn't have O'Neill doing somersaults either.

Indeed, at the end of match it is rumoured that the manager said to Rafael: "You can do everything I can do on the football pitch. Problem is, I'm 48."

O'Neill has never confirmed the veracity of the rumour, but if he didn't say it, he almost certainly thought it.

Things didn't get much better a few days later when Celtic flew to Denmark for a friendly against FC Copenhagen. Harald Brattbakk, a figure of fun for the misses he conjured up in a Celtic jersey, and of folklore for scoring the goal that ended Rangers' quest for 10-in-a-row in 1998, had left the club seven months earlier to play for Copenhagen.

Almost inevitably, the Norwegian scored two fabulous goals - the first again exploiting Rafael's lack of... well, everything really.

Two Mark Burchill goals earned Celtic a draw and while O'Neill was encouraged by the fighting spirit, he knew that Rafael was not the answer to his defensive prayers.

A third game was still to be played, bizarrely in Leipzig, Germany, against Third Division team Sachsen.

It was a game only noteworthy for the first appearance in the team of Chris Sutton, who had been signed for £6m earlier in the week and flew in to make his debut.

Celtic, though, were appalling. They lost the game 2-0 and afterwards the manager didn't try to hide his disappointment.

He said: "We are going to have to work when we get home because we have obvious defensive frailties.

"I spoke to the players after the match and told them they have to defend better all over the pitch. All the best sides do this and it is one of the reasons we are short.

"We have not defended properly as a team this week and I think the whole side needs improving all over the pitch."

A 4-2 defeat at the hands of Bordeaux in O'Neill's first outing at Parkhead wound up the preparation and further underlined the manager's doubts about Rafael.

When he picked his next team – for the SPL against Dundee

United – Rafael wasn't in it. He wasn't even on the bench and before long the Brazilian was back in his homeland on loan and has yet to re-emerge. It's doubtful if he ever will.

Celtic didn't miss him but the £5m hole in the club's bank balance is further proof of the mess the club was in before O'Neill chose to come to Parkhead.

SEVENTEEN

MARTIN O'NEILL'S first signing for Celtic was Chris Sutton from Chelsea, a player who was the Scottish record transfer fee at the time but who went on to justify the £6m price tag.

Sutton replaced the talented, but sometimes tormented, Mark Viduka and although the Englishman is not as prolific in front of goal as the Australian, he proved to be a better foil for Henrik Larsson who spent the season scoring at will.

O'Neill was keen to land Sutton from the minute Viduka told him in a tense, terse telephone call that he had no desire to continue playing for Celtic.

But the Chelsea attacker was not Martin's first signing target. Even before he accepted the Parkhead job, O'Neill knew that he wanted to take with him from Leicester City his midfield lynchpin Neil Lennon.

Lennon, by O'Neill's own admission, doesn't look much like a footballer. Then again, neither did John Robertson in his heyday and O'Neill knows just how brilliant his pal and assistant manager was on the other side of the pitch from him at Nottingham Forest.

He had plucked Lennon from the obscurity of Crewe Alexandria early in 1996 and watched the stocky midfielder drive Leicester City from the middle of the English First Division to the play-offs and then onto the Premiership.

That fire, determination and no little ability would be vital to Celtic as they tried to overhaul a Rangers team that had won the previous season's league title by 21 points.

A £7m bid was launched for Lennon within a couple of weeks of O'Neill's arrival, but the Filbert Street club – already sore at Celtic for taking their manager – wasn't going to give up their star player without a fight.

But O'Neill is nothing if not persistent and he kept nipping away at Leicester. He knew the player, like himself a Northern Irishman who had grown up in a family that were committed Celtic supporters had an insatiable desire to join him in Glasgow.

Lennon was persuaded to sign an extension to his Leicester City deal in an attempt by the club to ward off further overtures from O'Neill, but the Midlands outfit didn't really stand a chance because the player's heart was still set on moving.

Finally, early in December, Leicester boss Peter Taylor caved in and accepted Celtic's offer of around £6m. He cited as the reason: "Neil's obvious desperation to play for Celtic was affecting his training and preparation for Leicester matches."

Lennon would have wanted to play for Celtic no matter who was in the dug-out, but the fact that O'Neill, of all people, was there only reinforced his desire.

There might be almost 20 years between them but a mutual respect exists even if they don't spend much time in each other's company away from the pitch.

The empathy was obvious even on their first day together at Celtic Park, when facing the massed ranks of the media.

O'Neill guided Lennon, who looked perfectly capable of handling the occasion, through it like a nervous father.

He described his protege thus: "His biggest quality is that if a team needs pulling together, then Lennon's character will come through. He has the ability to link play from the back to the front. He's comfortable on the ball, won't give it away and can actually drop his shoulder and go past a few people.

"Don't be put off by the bulkiness of him (a remark that caused an eyebrow to be raised quizzically by Lennon) – he plays the game like he's two or three pounds overweight but there's not too many who go past him.

"I don't want to put ferocious pressure on him but if he doesn't do well, I'll kill him."

Also underscoring the ease they have in each other's company, there was a mockingly scolding reference to Lennon's preference of bleaching his ginger hair blond.

Lennon said: "That's been a massive problem for the last couple of years. I asked him why he did it and he said: 'To be different.' I said: 'Be different – score a hat-trick."

O'Neill knew exactly what he was getting when he signed the 29-year-old and in the week the championship was secured, the praise he heaped on Lennon could hardly have been higher.

He said: "I'd have no affinity with him whatsoever if he wasn't a very, very, good player for us and I wouldn't have brought him to this club if he wasn't.

"He's been terrific though. I know when he made his debut at Dundee some people thought he was a bit overweight and not quite fit.

"Even he couldn't believe the pace of the game up here. From that point on, however, he's adapted and he took on a big mantle when Paul Lambert was out injured.

"I think his contribution has been immense. When you talk about significant players, when we had Paul missing for that period of time, then whether we would even be in this position without Lennon is debatable.

"I have fantastic faith in him. I wanted him to dominate proceedings at Leicester and I want him to do the same here.

"He has the ability to make those five yard passes and the ability to take the sting out of a game. I have seldom seen him beaten for pace or trickery by players who are renowned for both.

"In the British game we look at people like Keane and Vieira. They are world class players and I am telling you Lennon aspires to that level and he's not far removed from it."

High praise indeed, but Lennon recalls a time when he wasn't the apple of O'Neill's eye.

He said: "I'd been sent off playing against Norwich City and he chased me up the tunnel to have a few words with me.

"It was my first game as captain, and needless to say, my last.

"You learn to regret these things and while I felt I had been hard done by with the decision, I was still hit with a hefty fine."

Lennon recalls meeting O'Neill for the first time when he was just a starstruck youngster looking for the Northern Ireland captain at the time's autograph.

His second meeting was much more important and paved the way for his career to really take off.

He said: "I was playing for Crewe and was living in a flat that looked like a scene from the Young Ones.

"I was on the verge of signing for Coventry City, but Martin and John Robertson turned up at the flat. He persuaded me there and then to sign for him and wrote out the contract on the back of a pizza box.

"John had watched me four or five times and Martin himself came along on three or four occasions because he likes to be sure of the players he signed.

"Martin is relentless and drives players on. He doesn't dazzle you with science, though. Everything is black and white and he doesn't ask anyone to do anything they can't.

"Just like at Leicester, everyone at this club is pulling in the same direction, from the players to the laundry ladies.

"If he had taken a big job earlier, no-one at Leicester could have grudged him it. I think it's a testiment to his loyalty that he stayed for as long as he did.

"Other people would definitely have walked away before he did and I think the people down there owe him a debt of gratitude.

"There are no grey areas with Martin. He's very up front with people and that's the way you want it.

"Obviously, he approached me in the summer and I knew there and then I wanted to come here.

"As soon as Martin got the job I had an inkling he'd come back in for me and everyone knows it has always been an ambition of mine to play for Celtic.

"But, at 29, I kept being told that I was getting long in the tooth, although I didn't see it that way, and it was just an opportunity I could not miss out on. It was the same for the manager. The offer to manage a club like Celtic was just too good to turn down."

Lennon has much to thank O'Neill for but has repaid his manager in the way he knows best. A player who has a radar-like knowledge of how to find a team-mate with the ball is always going to get pass marks.

EIGHTEEN

THEY rolled up in their thousands on March 18, 2001. Full of expectation rather than mere hope that this day would officially mark the beginning of a new era under Martin O'Neill.

They were not to be disappointed. The National Stadium at Hampden had been the scene of a £60m refurbishment not two years before but on this day it was to witness a one-man demolition.

Kilmarnock were the club sent crashing to their ground, their dreams of lifting the CIS Cup turned to dust by a wrecking ball going under the guise of an unassuming Swede.

A rainforest of newsprint has been used to describe Henrik Larsson's goalscoring exploits this season and his sense of timing, like his runs into the penalty box to get onto the end of team-mates' passes, tends to be immaculate.

When Celtic needed a big performance, Larsson always delivered and on the day of O'Neill's first cup final since coming to Scotland he didn't disappoint.

His two goals against Rangers in a stormy semi final that had been marred by an injury time brawl that saw Lubo Moravcik and Rangers pair Claudio Reyna and Michael Mols sent off, had paved the way for a final showdown with the Ayrshire club.

Celtic were leading the league by a comfortable distance and were hot favourites to retain the only trophy they won in the previous season under the caretaker managership of Kenny Dalglish.

But Kilmarnock were also going well, sitting fourth in the league, and they travelled to Hampden full of belief that they could win their second national trophy in four years, having won the Scottish Cup in 1997.

They might have done so, too, had it not been for Larsson.

The Ayrshire had given as good as they'd got in a first half that saw both sides losing vital players to injury. Bobby Petta had been risked despite missing the previous five matches but he lasted all of 12 minutes before a recurrence of his groin injury forced him to watch the rest of the match from the dug-out.

Kilmarnock's loss was perhaps even more significant. Their skipper Ian Durrant had also missed games in the run-up to the final because of a knee injury but for the first 35 minutes he was the most productive player on the pitch.

A simple twist on the Hampden turf was enough, however, to incur more damage on his knee ligaments and when Durrant was stretchered off, Kilmarnock's best hope departed with him.

Still, they reached the interval goalless but within two minutes of the restart Larsson had struck. The goal was Larsson's entire season in microcosm.

A corner was pinged into the box, Ramon Vega got the first touch with his head, Chris Sutton the second and as the ball bounced eight yards from goal everyone stood transfixed.

Well, everyone except Larsson. Anticipation, athleticism and adjustment were all displayed as he threw himself off the ground to meet the bouncing ball with a scissor kick. The ball blurred behind Gordon Marshall before the goalkeeper could move and Celtic were in front.

Sutton was sent off on the hour mark but under O'Neill Celtic teams take that kind of setback as a challenge rather than as an excuse to wilt.

They continued to pour forward and when Larsson latched onto a long ball and hit a shot off Chris Innes' leg to sent it looping over Marshall and into the net the final was over with 16 minutes remaining.

It was left only for the Swede to stamp his name all over the final with the completion of his hat-trick with 10 minutes left.

Picking up the ball on the halfway line, he brushed off Kevin McGowne en route to the penalty box where he casually rolled his studs over the ball to send Marshall one way and with a swing of the hips went the other.

The bodyswerve did more than beat the keeper - the 15,000 fans behind the goal also seemed to sway as he executed the manouevre.

A second later they were celebrating wildly as Henrik rolled the ball into the empty net.

So too was their manager. O'Neill knew the first trophy of his tenureship in the bag.

More importantly, the success meant more to the support than the CIS Cup victory of the previous season, which gave them one good night out in a season of misery.

This time it was different. The league was about to be won and the club remained in the Scottish Cup.

No, the winning of the 2000/2001 CIS Cup was a signal that Martin O'Neill had only just begun to do what he was brought to Glasgow to achieve - satisfy his club's craving for trophies.

ROUTE TO THE FINAL:

FOURTH ROUND - September 5, 2000: Celtic 4 (Thompson, Sutton, Johnson 2) Raith Rovers 0. Att: 30,753

Team: Kerr; Boyd, Valgaeren, Mahe; McNamara, Thompson, Healy, Petta (Tebily)(Rafael); Sutton (Berkovic), Johnson, Burchill

QUARTER FINAL - November 1, 2000: Hearts 2 (Cameron 2) Celtic 5 (McNamara, Moravcik, Healy, Crainey, Smith) Att: 13, 076

Team: Gould; Valgaeren, Riseth, Stubbs; McNamara, Thompson, Healy, Moravcik, Crainey (Petta); Johnson (Boyd), Smith (Petrov)

SEMI FINAL - February 7, 2001: Celtic 3 (Larsson 2, Sutton) Rangers 1 (Albertz) Att: 50,000

Team: Gould; Boyd, Mjallby, Vega; McNamara (Petta), Lambert, Lennon, Petrov, Thompson; Larsson (Moravcik), Sutton (Johnson)

FINAL - March 18, 2001: Celtic 3 (Larsson 3) Kilmarnock 0 Att: 48,830

Team: Gould; Valgaeren, Mjallby, Vega; Healy, Lambert, Lennon, Moravcik (Smith), Petta (Crainey)(Boyd); Sutton, Larsson.

WHILE Celtic steamrollered everything before them domestically, their European adventure came to a shuddering halt on a night of utter frustration at Parkhead against a very good Bordeaux side.

An excellent 1-1 first leg draw in the Stade Lescure, Henrik Larsson scoring Celtic's equaliser, had given Martin O'Neill genuine hope of making progress beyond the second round of the UEFA Cup.

When Lubo Moravcik shot Celtic in front in the return leg, to reward a period of almost constant pressure, their manager's confidence looked justified but an equaliser near the end from Bordeaux's French international striker Lilian Laslandes was enough to send the game into extra time.

The French, boosted by their late leveller, were more confident in the overtime period but the match was hurtling towards a penalty shoot-out when Laslandes struck again to silence the 51,000 crowd and end Celtic's hopes.

Earlier in the campaign Celtic had cruised the qualifying round, knocking 11 past Luxembourg's part-timers Jeunesse Esch without reply over the two matches.

A 4-0 win in Luxembourg, inspired by a dazzling display from Bobby Petta, rendered the second leg meaningless but that didn't stop more than 40,000 fans turning out to enjoy the seven goal romp, three of which were scored by Mark Burchill.

The first round proper was a tougher proposition altogether, although it really shouldn't have been. HJK Helsinki travelled to Glasgow for the first leg and shut up shop well enough to restrict the Scots to a 2-0 victory with Larsson notching both of them.

That should have been enough but a sloppy performance in Finland left Celtic hanging on by a thread. O'Neill's men lost goals either side of half time but early in extra time a close range strike from Chris Sutton put Celtic in the next round.

Next on the map was the visit to Bordeaux, where the adventure was to end. But Celtic's performance against a quality outfit was enough to convince O'Neill that his side was well equipped to handle the rigours of the domestic season. He wasn't wrong.

UEFA CUP RUN:

QUALIFIER FIRST LEG - Aug 10 - Jeunesse Esch 0 Celtic 4 (Moravcik 2, Larsson, Petta)

Team: Gould; McNamara (Healy), Mjallby, Valgaeren, Mahe; Lambert (Rafael), Riseth, Petta, Moravcik; Larsson (Johnson), Sutton

SECOND LEG - Aug 24 - Celtic 7 (Berkovic 2, Burchill 3, Riseth, Petrov) Jeunesse Esch 0

Team: Gould; Healy, Tebily, Rafael, Riseth; Lambert (Miller), Berkovic, Mjallby, Petta; Burchill (Boyd), Lynch (Petrov)

FIRST ROUND, FIRST LEG - Sept 14 - Celtic 2 (Larsson 2) HJK Helsinki 0

Team: Gould; Boyd, Valgaeren, Mjallby, Mahe (Healy); McNamara, Lambert, Petrov, Moravcik (Berkovic); Larsson, Sutton

SECOND LEG - SEPT 28 - HJK Helsinki 2 (Roiha 2) Celtic 1 (Sutton)

Team: Gould; McNamara (Moravcik), Boyd (Riseth), Valgaeren, Mjallby; Lambert, Petrov, Berkovic (Healy), Petta; Larsson, Sutton

SECOND ROUND FIRST LEG - OCT 26 - Bordeaux 1 (Dugarry) Celtic 1 (Larsson)

Team: Gould; McNamara, Boyd, Valgaeren, Mjallby; Agathe, Lambert, Petrov, Petta (Healy); Larsson, Moravcik

SECOND LEG - NOV 9 - Celtic 1 (Moravcik) Bordeaux 2 (Laslandes 2)

Team: Gould; McNamara (Healy) , Boyd, Valgaeren, Mjallby; Petrov, Petta (Berkovic), Agathe, Moravcik (Johnson); Larsson, Sutton

NINETEEN

SUNDAY, July 30, and the footballing world – or at least the areas of it that Sky's cameras penetrate – waited and wondered if Martin O'Neill had been able to make an immediate impact at Celtic.

The Irishman had taken his team to Tannadice for the first game of their SPL campaign and after a stuttering pre-season build-up, many were asking if the club was to begin the campaign as ignominiously as it had ended the last.

It didn't take long to find out.

Within 37 minutes Henrik Larsson had scored the first of the barrowload he was to collect throughout the course of the season but the real test was to come just four minutes after the break when David McCracken equalised. The previous season, such an occurance would have led to a cave in and the loss of a second goal.

But with O'Neill badgering them from the sidelines, Celtic dug in. They hassled and harried and got their reward when Chris Sutton scored his first goal for the club. Celtic won 2-1 and were off and running.

JULY 30: Dundee Utd 1 (McCracken) Celtic 2 (Larsson, Sutton)

Celtic: Gould, Boyd, Mahe, Valgaeren, Stubbs; Berkovic, McNamara, Lambert, Petrov, Sutton, Larsson.

Six days later O'Neill's first league outing at home attracted 58,534 to Parkhead and they witnessed a hard fought affair that was decided by Bulgarian internationalist Stilian Petrov's early goal.

Interestingly, O'Neill had started each match with the mercurial Eyal Berkovic in his line-up but the Israeli had failed to shine and by the time league game number three came up, the midfielder was out and Bobby Petta – almost forgotten during the previous John Barnes-Kenny Dalglish reign – was in.

Not only in, but bang in form and looking nothing like the confidence-shredded winger of the previous season. Kilmarnock were the visitors to Parkhead and signalled their intentions with a sensational early strike from Andy McLaren but again Celtic showed their mettle, coming back to win with second half strikes from Larsson and Tommy Johnson.

Maximum points from the first three games had Celtic fans praying that this would be their season but the next 180 minutes turned hope into expectation.

Their team travelled to Tynecastle and played Hearts off the park, scoring three times in the first half through Sutton twice and Larsson before Lubo Moravcik added a fourth. Hearts scored twice in the latter stages through Scott Severin and Juanjo but those strikes were merely consolation for the well beaten Edinburgh side.

Eight days later, Celtic hammered Rangers in O'Neill's first Old Firm derby and there and then everyone within the club started believing. Really believing.

Sutton got the ball rolling with a goal in the first minute and added a second in injury time. In between, Celtic pillaged the Rangers defence on another four occasions through Petrov, Paul Lambert and a Larsson double, the first of which was a simply sublime piece of skill to outpace Bert Konterman and chip Stefan Klos.

Rangers scored twice through Claudio Reyna and Billy Dodds but it was never going to be enough and for their young skipper Barry Ferguson a 6-2 defeat was all too much and he was sent off near the end.

The Celtic support celebrated the victory like there was no tomorrow and O'Neill tried hard to keep a lid on the euphoria, knowing full well that it was too early to be talking titles.

Nevertheless, Celtic had laid down their marker for the season and Rangers failed to pick it up.

AUGUST RESULTS

AUGUST 5: Celtic 1 (Petrov) Motherwell 0

Team: Gould, Boyd, Mahe, Tebily, Valgaeren; Berkovic (Mjallby), Lambert, McNamara, Petrov; Sutton, Larsson.

AUGUST 13: Celtic 2 (Larsson, Johnson) Kilmarnock 1 (McLaren).

Team: Gould, Boyd (Mjallby), Mahe, Stubbs, Valgaeren; Lambert, Moravcik, Petta, Petrov; Johnson, Larsson

AUGUST 19: Hearts 2 (Severin, Juanjo) Celtic 4 (Sutton 2, Larsson, Moravcik)

Team: Gould, Mahe, Stubbs (Mjallby), Valgaeren; Lambert, McNamara, Moravcik (Boyd), Petrov, Petta; Larsson, Sutton.

AUGUST 27: Celtic 6 (Sutton 2, Larsson 2, Lambert, Petrov) Rangers 2 (Reyna, Dodds)

Team: Gould; Mahe, Stubbs, Valgaeren; Lambert (Mjallby), McNamara, Moravcik (Boyd), Petrov, Petta; Larsson, Sutton.

THREE more wins were recorded on the spin in September – a 3-0 demolition of Hibernian at Parkhead with goals from Larsson (2) and Mark Burchill was followed by a fortuitious victory at East End Park when a late Larsson goal, his second of the night, was enough to beat Steve Crawford's penalty for Dunfermline.

Petrov's influence was growing with every match and for the second time in the first eight games the Bulgarian scored the only goal – this time an hour into a tense affair against Dundee.

SEPTEMBER RESULTS

SEPT 9: Celtic 3 (Larsson 2, Burchill) Hibs 0

Team: Gould; Boyd, Stubbs (Mjallby), Valgaeren; Lambert, McNamara, Moravcik (Burchill), Petrov; Larsson, Sutton.

SEPT 18: Dunfermline 1 (Crawford) Celtic 2 (Larsson 2)

Team: Gould; Boyd, Mahe (Moravcik), Mjallby, Valgaeren; Lambert, McNamara, Petrov, Thompson; Larsson, Sutton.

SEPT 23: Celtic 1 (Petrov) Dundee 0

Team: Gould; Boyd, Mjallby, Valgaeren; Lambert, McNamara, Moravcik (Stubbs), Petrov, Thompson(Healy); Larsson, Sutton

ABERDEEN was the next hurdle to be negotiated on the first day of October and Pittodrie was the place where Celtic had their first stumble of the season, spilling two points.

It would have been worse but for Larsson's late strike, which cancelled out Robbie Winters' first half goal.

Still, a draw after eight straight wins was hardly going to have O'Neill reaching for the panic button.

By the time Celtic's next match came round, however, on

October 14, the Irishman had another weapon in his armoury –
Didier Agathe.

O'Neill didn't emerge from Easter Road in the dead of night
wearing a mask and a stripey jumper, carrying a swag bag
containing the Frenchman over his shoulder. But nonetheless, the
£50,000 fee that took Agathe from Hibs was to become the steal
of the season.

Agathe made his league debut against St Mirren but it was the
rapidly flourishing partnership of Sutton and Larsson that grabbed
the goals in the 2-0 home win.

That scoreline was repeated on the road just three days later,
goals from Joos Valgaeren and Larsson seeing off St Johnstone at
McDiarmid Park.

A 2-1 win over Dundee United at Parkhead was a lot more
comfortable than the scoreline suggests, with Larsson and Alan
Thompson putting Celtic in control long before Lambert scuffed
an own goal beyond Jonathan Gould.

The team rounded off the month as it had started it, by dropping
two points on opposition soil. They travelled to Motherwell and
were involved in a cracking 3-3 draw, which Celtic believe should
have been a 4-3 victory. Given that Johan Mjallby, who had given
Celtic the lead, had a second effort cleared when it was obviously
over the line, you could see their point.

Celtic's three goals came from unusual sources - Valgaeren and
McNamara adding to Mjallby's counter but Motherwell's workrate
and goals from Don Goodman, Ged Brannan and Greg Strong
gave them a share of the spoils.

OCTOBER RESULTS:

OCT 1: Aberdeen 1 (Winters) Celtic 1 (Larsson)
 Team: Gould; Boyd, Mjallby, Valgaeren; Lambert (Moravcik),
McNamara, Petrov, Petta, Thompson (Mahe) (Healy); Larsson,
Sutton.

OCT 14: Celtic 2 (Sutton, Larsson) St Mirren 0
 Team: Gould; Boyd, Mjallby, Valgaeren; Lambert, Moravcik
(Riseth), Petrov (Healy), Thompson, Agathe; Larsson, Sutton.

OCT 17: St Johnstone 0 Celtic 2 (Valgaeren, Larsson)
 Team: Gould, Boyd, Mjallby, Valgaeren; Lambert, Petrov (Healy),
Petta, Thompson, Agathe; Larsson, Sutton

OCT 21: Celtic 2 (Larsson, Thompson) Dundee Utd 1(Lambert og)
 Team: Gould; Boyd, Mjallby, Valgaeren, Lambert, Petrov, Petta
(McNamara), Thompson, Agathe; Larsson, Sutton

OCT 29: Motherwell 3 (Goodman, Brannan, Strong) Celtic 3

(Mjallby, Valgaeren, McNamara)

Team: Gould, Boyd, Mjallby (Stubbs), Valgaeren; Lambert, McNamara, Petrov, Petta, Thompson; Agathe (Moravcik), Larsson

THERE weren't many fireworks at Rugby Park on November 5 but Alan Thompson's goal kept Celtic's championship ambitions burning brightly and although disappointment was to follow in Europe in midweek – O'Neill's men lost in extra time to Bordeaux – the team immediately bounced back against St Johnstone at Parkhead.

Goalkeeper Rab Douglas had been signed from Dundee a few weeks earlier, but his ineligibility for Europe had given Jonathan Gould a stay of executive until their exit.

Now it was Douglas' turn to step into the limelight and he would have disappointed to lose a goal to Saints' Craig Russell, even if it didn't affect the result because Celtic were cruising at 4-0 when the Englishman scored.

Goals from Sutton, Larsson (2) and Moravcik set Celts up for their next match and Hearts had the misfortune to run into them just as they hit top gear.

Colin Cameron had given the visitors the lead completely against the run of play but when Valgaeren grabbed the equaliser the floodgates opened and another five flew past Antti Niemi, who prevented the home side reaching double figures with an inspired display.

Inevitably, Larsson got a double with Mjallby, Petrov and Moravcik weighing in with the others.

The performance was devastating and send Celtic to Ibrox the following week full of confidence. A win would make it very difficult for Rangers to overhaul them, even though the campaign hadn't reached December.

What followed was the worst day of O'Neill's reign. Rangers, smarting from their earlier drubbing at Parkhead, ran out 5-1 winners, taking advantage of Thompson's red card when the score was 2-1.

Larsson's headed equaliser, after Barry Ferguson had given Rangers the lead, gave them hope but Ronald de Boer, Lorenzo Amoruso, Tore Andre Flo and Michael Mols gave the Ibrox side their revenge.

Much would now depend on how Celtic bounced back and their next match, just three days later was at Easter Road, where Hibs were having a sensational season.

Celtic couldn't afford to lose two in a row and they grit their teeth and ground out a goalless draw that steadied the ship. It was also to be the last point they conceded until Hibs came to their place ten league games later at the end of February.

NOVEMBER RESULTS:

NOV 5: Kilmarnock 0 Celtic 1 (Thompson)

Team: Gould; Boyd, Mjallby, Valgaeren; Lambert (Agathe), McNamara, Petrov (Healy), Petta, Thompson; Larsson, Sutton

NOV 12: Celtic 4 (Sutton, Larsson 2, Moravcik) St Johnstone 1(Russell)

Team: Douglas; Mjallby, Stubbs, Valgaeren; Moravcik, Petrov (Healy), Petta, Thompson, Agathe; Larsson, Sutton (Johnson)

NOV 18: Celtic 6 (Valgaeren, Mjallby, Larsson 2, Petrov, Moravcik) Hearts 1 (Cameron)

Team: Douglas; Boyd, Mjallby (Tebily), Valgaeren; Moravcik, Petrov, Petta, Thompson, Agathe; Larsson, Sutton (Johnson)

NOV 26: Rangers 5 (Ferguson, de Boer, Amoruso, Flo, Mols) Celtic 1 (Larsson)

Team: Douglas; Boyd, Mjallby (McNamara), Valgaeren; Moravcik (Mahe), Petrov, Petta, Thompson, Agathe; Larsson, Sutton (Johnson)

NOV 29: Hibs 0 Celtic 0

Team: Douglas; Boyd, Mjallby, Valgaeren; Healy (Moravcik), McNamara, Petrov, Petta (Mahe), Agathe; Larsson, Sutton.

THE point at Easter Road had restored the team's confidence and although they lost an early goal in their next outing against Dunfermline at Parkhead, they bounced back to win by a comfortable 3-1 margin.

Larsson was scoring at will, and sure enough he got the third of the afternoon to set the seal on the platform that been built by Moravcik and Johnson's earlier strikes.

A major result was eked out eight days later when a last gasp Agathe goal – his first for the club – gave Celtic an ill-deserved but welcome victory over Dundee at Dens Park after Tom Boyd had steered a header beyond his own keeper to nullify Petrov's opener.

The other significant factor that night was the debut of Neil Lennon, who had been sought by O'Neill almost since the day he left Leicester. The manager wanted his former Filbert Street star and finally persuaded his old club to part with the Northern Ireland internationalist in a £6m deal.

If the Dundee result was tight, the following match was a stroll and a night of triumph for Ramon Vega, who had been brought in from Spurs to stiffen the defence.

It was in Aberdeen's area that the big Swiss made an immediate impact, blasting home two headers as Celtic romped to a 6-0 win. Larsson, not to be outdone, scored a hat-trick with young Jamie Smith coming off the bench to grab another.

The bandwagon rolled onto Love Street, two days before Christmas, and a functional if not flamboyant 2-0 win was secured with goals from Agathe and Larsson.

They were much more impressive on Boxing Day, leaving Dundee United punch drunk with a four-goal barrage at Tannadice with Sutton grabbing two, Larsson one and Petrov the other.

Celtic ended the year top of the pile by a mile and looking certs for the title even if O'Neill continued to deny it.

DECEMBER RESULTS:

DEC 2: Celtic 3 (Moravcik, Johnson, Larsson) Dunfermline 1 (Dair)

Team: Douglas, Boyd, Mjallby, Valgaeren; Moravcik (McNamara), Petrov, Petta, Thompson, Agathe; Johnson, Larsson

DEC 10: Dundee 1 (Boyd og) Celtic 2 (Petrov, Agathe)

Team: Douglas; Boyd, Mjallby, Valgaeren; Moravcik (McNamara), Petrov, Petta, Thompson, Lennon; Agathe, Larsson

DEC 16: Celtic 6 (Vega 2, Larsson 3, Smith) Aberdeen 0

Team: Douglas; Valgaeren, Mjallby, Vega; Lennon, Petrov, Petta, Thompson, Agathe; Johnson (Smith), Larsson

DEC 23: St Mirren 0 Celtic 2 (Agathe, Larsson)

Team: Douglas, Valgaeren, Mjallby, Vega; Lennon, Petrov, Petta (McNamara), Thompson, Agathe; Sutton, Larsson

DEC 26: Dundee Utd 0 Celtic 4 (Larsson, Sutton 2, Petrov)

Team: Douglas, Valgaeren, Mjallby, Vega; Lennon, McNamara, Petrov (Smith), Petta (Moravcik), Agathe; Larsson (Johnson), Sutton.

MAXIMUM points from December sent Celtic into 2001 on a high and Kilmarnock were the team that felt the full force of their belief that they were on the verge of something special.

Bobby Williamson's team came to Parkhead on January 2 confidently enough, they were, after all, fourth in the table and going well. But by the end of 90 torrid minutes they had been run ragged.

Yet again, the Larsson-Sutton partnership proved too hot to handle and although the Englishman kicked off the rout with the first goal, it was the Swede who again grabbed the attention by knocking four past Gordon Marshall.

Sutton added his own second and for the fourth time in the league season, Celtic had hit an opponent for six.

The squad hardly needed a jet to carry them on their mid-winter break to Florida a week later. They were flying on their own.

JANUARY RESULTS

JAN 2: Celtic 6 (Sutton 2, Larsson 4) Kilmarnock 0

Team: Douglas, Mjallby, Valgaeren, Vega; Lennon, McNamara (Moravcik), Petrov (Smith), Petta (Thompson), Agathe; Sutton, Larsson

O'NEILL and his men returned from the States fully refreshed but their opponents wondered if their momentum had been disrupted by the month off. It took them 90 minutes to dispell that notion and Hearts were the team who suffered.

Larsson picked up where he left off and bagged a hat-trick at Tynecastle in a match that also gave O'Neill the luxury of fielding fit again Lambert, whose injured ankle had kept him out since November, in the same midfield as Lennon for the first time.

Rangers, meanwhile, had been lurching from one crisis to the next but were still held hope of catching Celtic as they prepared for a win or bust mission at Parkhead on February 11.

The third meeting of the season was more a war of attrition than a free-flowing festival of football but Celtic got their noses in front early through Thompson and refused to give any ground to their rivals.

Their fans celebrated the 1-0 win as they would a title victory, and the disconsolate look in the faces of the Rangers players as they trooped off indicated that they, too, knew it was all over.

Celtic, though, had still to cross the finishing line and they took another three steps towards that with another hard fought, edgy, win over Motherwell at Parkhead. The Fir Park side defended as if their lives depended on it but with seven minutes remaining Moravcik rattled a 20 yard free kick high past Andy Goram to secure another vital victory.

Celtic's final outing of the month was significant in that it saw them drop their first league points of the season at Parkhead.

Hibs, who were still in contention to split the Old Firm at the time, arrived in Glasgow full of belief and it was borne out by a late equaliser from debutant Marco Libbra, who cancelled out Mjallby's earlier strike.

The damage to Celtic's title hopes was, however, minimal. They had enjoyed another superb month.

FEBRUARY RESULTS

FEB 4: Hearts 0 Celtic 3 (Larsson 3)

Team: Douglas; Mjallby, Valgaeren, Vega; Lambert, Lennon, McNamara, Thompson, Agathe; Sutton, Larsson.

FEB 11: Celtic 1 (Thompson) Rangers 0

Team: Douglas; Boyd, Mjallby (Tebily), Vega; Lennon, Lambert, Petta, Thompson, Agathe; Larsson, Sutton

FEB 21: Celtic 1 (Moravcik) Motherwell 0

Team: Douglas; Mjallby, Valgaeren (Boyd), Vega; Lennon, Lambert (Moravcik), Petta (Petrov), Thompson, Agathe; Larsson, Sutton

FEB 25: Celtic 1 (Mjallby) Hibs 1 (Libbra)

Team: Douglas; Boyd, Mjallby, Vega; Lennon, Lambert, Petrov, Thompson, Agathe; Larsson, Sutton

CUP competitions held much of Celtic's interest in March – they were to win their first trophy under O'Neill by lifting the CIS Cup on the 18th – but two league games were completed and yet again, maximum points were secured.

Dunfermline were disposed of in fine fashion at End Park, with Lennon grabbing his first goal for the club to supplement earlier strikes from Petrov and Larsson.

Ten days later another win was achieved, but this time at a dreadful price. A 2-1 win over St Johnstone in Perth was marred by a broken leg sustained in the dying minutes by Petrov.

MARCH RESULTS

MAR 4: Dunfermline 0 Celtic 3 (Petrov, Larsson, Lennon)

Team: Douglas; Valgaeren, Vega, Mjallby; Lennon (Crainey), Lambert, Petrov, Thompson, Agathe; Larsson, Sutton (Johnson)

MAR 14: St Johnstone 1 (McCluskey) Celtic 2 (Johnson, Larsson)

Team: Douglas; Mjallby, Valgaeren, Vega; Lennon, Petrov (Crainey), Lambert, Thompson, Agathe; Larsson, Johnson

THE first day of April saw Celtic go back to Aberdeen knowing that within the space of a week the title could be theirs.

Rangers had lost again, the previous day, leaving O'Neill's team needing nine points from three games – all to be played in six days.

Part one was at Pittodrie and although it was an almighty struggle, the visitors prevailed with an Agathe goal deep into the second half. One down and two to go because two down and one to go the following midweek when Dundee came to town and were beaten 2-1 thanks to a scrambled late goal from Mjallby.

Johnson had given the home team the lead but Juan Sara had wiped it out after the break and for a long time it seemed that Saturday's clash with St Mirren would not, after all, be the day the title was clinched.

Mjallby's late winner changed all that and at lunchtime on April 7 – the kick off brought forward to accomodate pay-per-view television – Celtic took the field knowing a win would be enough for the party to begin.

The nervousness within the ranks, given the size of the prize, was understandable, and not even Johnson's goal in 37 minutes from the break settled the butterflies.

A second goal would have, but it didn't come and although St Mirren had a few flurries around Douglas' goal, the party spoiler didn't come.

The final whistle did, eventually, and the celebrations could begin.

The league was over even before the much vaunted SPL split came into effect. With five games remaining, the party was over for 11 clubs. For one it was just starting.

And it continued 15 days later when Hearts came to Celtic Park and were unable to prevent Moravcik coming off the bench to score the only goal of the game midway through the second half. The SPL trophy was presented to Tom Boyd at the end of the match and the celebrations continued long into the night.

The party continued all the way to the Ibrox the following Sunday when O'Neill's men recorded their first win at the home of Rangers since 1994.

Two goals from the evergreen Moravcik and Larsson's 50th strike of the season near the end of the match sent the Celtic support into ecstacy and stretched their lead at the top of the table to 21 points - the same total as they'd lost the league the previous season.

APRIL RESULTS:

APR 1: Aberdeen 0 Celtic 1 (Agathe)
Team: Douglas; Mjallby, Valgaeren, Vega; Healy (McNamara), Lambert, Lennon (Moravcik), Thompson, Agathe; Johnson, Larsson

APR 4: Celtic 2 (Johnson, Mjallby) Dundee 1 (Sara)
Team: Douglas; Mjallby, Valgaeren, Vega; Lennon, Lambert, Thompson, Agathe, Moravcik (Boyd); Johnson, Larsson

APR 7: Celtic 1 (Johnson) St Mirren 0
Team: Douglas; Valgaeren (Boyd), Mjallby, Vega; Lennon, Lambert, Moravcik (Healy), Thompson, Agathe; Larsson, Johnson (McNamara)

APR 22: Celtic 1 (Moravcik) Hearts 0
Team: Douglas; Valgaeren, Mjallby, Vega; Healy (Moravcik), Lambert (Boyd), McNamara, Thompson, Agathe; Johnson (Smith), Larsson

APR 29: Rangers 0 Celtic 3 (Moravcik 2, Larsson)
Team: Douglas; Valgaeren, Mjallby, Vega; Lambert (Boyd), Lennon, Moravcik (McNamara), Thompson, Agathe; Johnson (Maloney), Larsson

Alan Stubbs had won a more important battle than any ever fought on a football field – for survival against testicular cancer that had struck twice.

On May 6, the Celtic defender made his first team comeback at Easter Road and delighted all by scoring as his team cruised to a 5-2 victory. Jackie McNamara had started the rout with a double, followed by Henrik Larsson equalling the Premier League scoring record of 35 in a season and Lubo Moravcik continuing his rich vein of form with another fine goal.

Didier Agathe was red carded near the end and as Celtic switched off, Hibs grabbed two consolations from Marc Libbra.

If Celtic had switched off near the end at Easter Road, they carried on in the same vein the following Sunday against Dundee, where their proud unbeaten home record was ruined by two goals from the Tayside team's Argentinian striker Fabian Caballero.

With the league won, the motivation seemed to have gone and Celtic would have to wait until the last game of the season to try to hit the 100 point mark against Kilmarnock.

They failed to do so at Rugby Park, losing the game 1-0 but prompting criticism for fielding a weakened team in order to rest players ahead of the following week's Scottish Cup Final.

The result meant that Killie staved off Hearts' attempts to wrest the final UEFA Cup place from them and left several Tynecastle players complaining that O'Neill had showed a lack of respect by leaving out nine regular first team players.

O'Neill insisted it was his job to prepare his own team properly for the cup final rather than worry about other clubs. No Celtic fan would have disagreed.

MAY RESULTS:

MAY 6: Hibs 2 (Libbra 2) Celtic 5 (McNamara 2, Larsson, Stubbs, Moravcik)

Team: Kharine; Boyd, Vega, Valgaraen (Stubbs), Vega; Agathe, Lennon (Healy), Lambert (Maloney), Thompson, McNamara; Moravcik, Larsson

MAY 13: Celtic 0 Dundee 2 (Caballero 2)

Team: Gould; Valgaeren (Stubbs), Mjallby, Vega (Boyd); McNamara, Thompson, Lennon, Lambert, Moravcik; Smith (Maloney), Larsson

MAY 20: Kilmarnock 1 (Mahood) Celtic 0

Team: Douglas; Boyd, Stubbs, Vega, Tebily; McNamara, Healy, Fotheringham, Mahe; Maloney, Smith

WHEN the dust had settled, O'Neill was able to reflect on the games that pointed his team in the direction of the title. Their sheer consistency, of course, was a major factor in their romp to the title but O'Neill recognised specific matches as being particularly important.

He said: "I can go all the way back to the very first league game of the season when we went to Tannadice for the match against Dundee United.

"I hadn't been here for very long and it taught me that the players were willing to work hard for any success we were to get.

"We won the match 2-1 after being pegged back to 1-1 and after that we went to win the next few games to get off to a good start.

"Of course, the first Old Firm game was important as well and it was a big one to win. The result gave us the confidence to know that maybe we could keep up a challenge to Rangers.

"A lot was made of the fact we won the game 6-2 but that was my only thought at the time.

"Another massive match for us was right after the mid-winter break when we went to Tynecastle and won 3-0 with a hat-trick from Henrik.

"Rangers had played and won the previous day and had reduced to the gap between us to just six points, which I honestly believed to be nothing at all at that stage.

"The pressure was on and we had to go to Tynecastle and respond in the proper manner, which we did. It was a big result.

"Another one was the home win over Motherwell in February just a few days after we had beaten Rangers. Many people thought the Rangers result was important, and it was, but it was crucial to follow it up with another win in midweek and for a long time the goal didn't look like coming.

"Then Lubo stepped up to hit a free kick into the net with seven minutes to go and we had another victory. In the context of things it was vital."

TWENTY

THE memory of the previous season's inglorious Scottish Cup exit at the hands of Inverness Caledonian Thistle still stabbed at the Celtic support like a stiletto through the heart.

The result, though, sparked off the chain of events that had led to Martin O'Neill receiving the call to lead the club out of the darkness into which they had been plunged in the wake of John Barnes' disastrous stewardship.

Come January, and the start of the new Scottish Cup campaign, O'Neill had his feet well and truly under the manager's desk and his talismanic qualities were already coming to the fore.

His team was leading the league by a comfortable margin, it was still in the CIS Cup and although their European adventure had come to an end against Bordeaux, there was still reason to believe that the club was moving in the right direction more quickly than anyone dared believe was possible.

The draw for the third round of the Scottish Cup, though, was exactly the type to bring back memories of the previous year.

Celtic were paired with Second Division Stranraer at Stair Park, which is exactly the kind of breeding ground for a cup upset that Sky television loves, so they sent their cameras to the tiny 5600 stadium, which is filled to bursting point with excited locals and the Celtic supporters who had made the long journey in good cheer and maybe, just maybe, a little trepidation.

They needn't have worried. Sky's hopes of beaming a sensation live to the nation were knocked out by a four goal Celtic blitz, started by Joos Valgaeren and added to by McNamara and the unfortunate Keith Knox who slotted into his own net.

Stranraer did grab a late consolation through Ian Harty and it was one that nobody but goalkeeper Rab Douglas could really grudge them. Moravcik added Celtic's fourth in the dying minutes to seal a professional performance. The ghost of Inverness Caley Thistle had been laid to rest.

The fourth round saw Celtic on their travels again, this time to a potentially more dangerous tie against Dunfermline at East End Park.

One of the most thrilling games of the season ended in a 2-2 draw courtesy of a last gasp strike from Dunfermline's former Rangers midfielder Barry Nicholson. Three goals in the last 10 minutes lit up the match that Celtic had led through Larsson's 67th minute goal but Andrius Skerla cancelled that out and when Henrik hit his second of the game with just three minutes left, it seemed Celtic were home and dry. Nicholson's injury time strike meant they had to win it all over again at home on March 7.

Two goals from Ramon Vega and another two from Larsson sent O'Neill's men into the quarter finals where Hearts lay in wait. Scott Thomson scored for the Pars but it was scant consolation.

The Tynecastle side came to Parkhead, defended well, but offered little up front and paid the price. A single Larsson goal was enough to end their resistance and set Celts up for a semi final showdown with Dundee United.

The Tannadice team fought relegation all season but had put together a cup run that included the scalp of Rangers - but at Hampden they found Larsson in irrestistable form. The Swede scored twice, McNamara added another and United were well beaten before Derek Lilley grabbed their late consolation.

Celtic were in the final of the Tennent's Scottish Cup. Hibs would join them at Hampden and if they were to be beaten the Treble would be at Parkhead for the first time since 1969.

ROUTE TO THE FINAL:
THIRD ROUND - JAN 28 - Stranraer 1 (Harty) Celtic 4 (Valgaeren, McNamara, Knox og, Moravcik)
Team: Douglas; Valgaeren (Mjallby), Vega, Boyd; McNamara,

Thompson, Lennon, Petta (Lambert), Agathe; Larsson (Moravcik), Sutton

FOURTH ROUND - FEB 17 - Dunfermline 2 (Skerla, Nicholson) Celtic 2 (Larsson 2)

Team: Douglas; Boyd, Valgaeren (Tebily), Vega; Lennon, Lambert, Thompson, Agathe, Petta (Petrov); Sutton, Larsson

FOURTH ROUND REPLAY - MAR 7 - Celtic 4 (Larsson 2, Vega 2) Dunfermline 1 (Thomson)

Team: Douglas; Valgaeren, Mjallby, Vega; McNamara (Petrov) Thompson, Lennon, Moravcik, Petta; Larsson (Crainey), Johnson (Lambert)

QUARTER FINAL - MAR 11 - Celtic 1 (Larsson) Hearts 0

Team: Douglas; Valgaeren, Mjallby (Boyd), Vega; Lambert, Lennon, Petrov, Thompson, Agathe; Moravcik (Johnson), Larsson

SEMI FINAL - APR 15 - Celtic 3 (Larsson 2, McNamara), Dundee Utd 1 (Lilley)

Team: Douglas; Valgaeren, Mjallby (Boyd), Vega; Lambert, Lennon, Thompson, Moravcik (McNamara), Agathe; Larsson, Sutton (Johnson)

TWENTY ONE

ANOTHER match had been won, another opponent banished and Martin O'Neill walked into another packed Press conference to give his verdict on his team's performance.

Before he could utter a word, the wearer of a green and white scarf, conspicious among the suits, stood up and in a quivering voice did not ask a question, but uttered a simple statement straight from the heart that was undoubtedly beating like a drum.

"Martin, I just want to thank you fur givin' us back wur pride."

Somehow the supporter had infiltrated the Press conference and while one or two of the assembled media frowned upon the interruption – they did, after all, have a job to do – the moment was, neverthless, a poignant one.

This one fan, a middle aged man who had without doubt suffered throughout the years of famine when Rangers stacked up trophy after trophy, was speaking for the 60,000 who couldn't gatecrash the press conference.

O'Neill's gift is not only his ability to make football players give him everything they possess in terms of skill, vision and effort.

He also has a Svengali-like sway over the Celtic support as those who partied in the streets of the East End of the city on the day Celtic won the league would testify.

There were at least 15,000 of them, a sea of green and white, as they invaded the Royston and Garngad housing scheme for the biggest street party Scotland had ever seen.

In every corner jubilant fans did the famous Celtic huddle, grown men tearfully told each other they could die happy now that this was their finest moment.

Celtic fanatic, Joe Chambers, 39, who organised the party said it was one of the best nights of his life.

He said: "It started with an idea to have a bit of a street party, but it snowballed into something unbelievable.

"Everyone who left Celtic park that day wanted to be with their own people and more and more people poured into the Garngad than I had ever seen before.

"It was as if we had waited so long for this sucess that we didn't want the night to end."

For Joe and the hordes of Celtic fans like him, Martin O'Neill has become their saviour.

Week in week out, they gather in the famous Baird's Bar in the east end airing their pre-match hopes and afterwards their post mortem on the game.

But it wasn't always like that.

Last season Baird's Bar was where then caretaker manager Kenny Dalglish decided to hold press conferences in a stunt that he claimed was intended to make the Celtic punter more involved.

But it was more widely believed that it was an attempt to bring the press into line, believing that if the press were little intimidated in a diehard Celtic pub they would be less to ask awkward questions about thorny issues.

It backfired and looked more and more awkward each time the press conferences were held. There seemed to be a lack of understanding by the management of Celtic that the club is more important than a cheap publicity stunt.

To the people who frequent Baird's Bar and the others around it, Celtic is a way of life, a belief, and even in some cases a religion.

Now, walk into the bar any match day and all you see are smiling faces of people who have been given something to live for.

Joe Chambers said: "I come from a long line of Celtic fans. I never miss a home game. I went through the time when Celtic fans were walking out and I never agreed with that.

"It is more than football to me. When my boys were growing up I used to say to them that if they went out wearing a Celtic jersey then they had to behave themselves at all times because they were representing the club and anything they did would reflect on the club. I know it sounds ridiculous, but that's how I feel about it.

"It is like a religion to me. I go to mass on a Sunday and I go to Parkhead on a Saturday. We worship different Gods on different days."

Outside his home, Joe hoists three flags up the 25ft flag pole for each home game. The three flags are a tricolour, a league championship flage, and, of course, the Swedish flag of his hero Henrik Larsson.

He said Martin O'Neill has given Celtic fans more pride than they believed possible.

Joe said: "There have been times when Celtic took up 50% of my life. I had a green room done up in my son's room and people used to come and visit it. My life was dedicated to Celtic.

"Martin O'Neill has given us the pride to walk out of the door in the morning. Even if we don't do it again next season, we have done it. The way it has gone this season with Rangers, we have taken everything.

"Last year Rangers were 21 points ahead of Celtic and as Martin O'Neill said, you don't win by that kind of margin and not be a good team. But because of him we have taken the 21 points back, we have taken the league the CIS, and the Scottish Cup. Larsson broke his record at Ibrox. The only thing we haven't taken off Rangers is that they have been able to secure a place in Europe.

"Martin O'Neill is one of the most genuine managers we have had. His Irish background and the fact that he is a lifelong Celtic fan. When John Barnes was there, he was trying his best, but you got the feeling it didn't mean that much to him. Martin O'Neill is like my second God."

Winning the league championship was a huge watershed for the Celtic fans who have lived through the miserable years of defeat at the club.

But as he explained, even when the club won the championship in 1998, there was still a sense of foreboding around Celtic park.

Peter Rafferty, chairman of the Affiliation of Registered Celtic Supporters:

"If you are a fan you have to accept the good times and the bad times. I was fortunate enough to see the great times in the 60s and 70s under Jock Stein. We had sporadic success in between that and there were difficult times for a while.

"When Fergus McCann came things improved such as the stadium and the finances got better. Fans put in £13.2 million to help turn the club's finances around and were playing a major part. But on the field of play things were difficult for us.

"During the barren times, Wim Jansen helped us stop Rangers winning 10 in a row and it was a memorable time. The last few days just crossing the line there was so much tension on the field and in the stand, but we broke through. But by the Monday, Jansen had resigned so we never really got an opportunity to enjoy the feeling of winning the championship during the summer months.

"The political climate at Celtic seemed to be difficult at that time. There always seemed to be another agenda taking place which seemed to interrupt or interfere with what we were trying to do on the field of play.

"When Jo Vengloss came we had a horrendous season winning nothing, then John Barnes Kenny Dalglish era. I think it was a bad mistake appointing Barnes as head coach. He didn't have the experience, knowledge or background to know what Celtic is all about. Celtic is a huge club and it became a baptism of fire for him.

"Kenny obviously did have that experience to manage a club like Celtic and we did win something, but there was a great deal of unrest and the dressing room seemed to be lost."

The arrival of O'Neill was talked about by Celtic fans for weeks before he finally stood before them on the steps of Celtic park.

Peter said: "Before Martin arrived we had spoken many times about him. Our association organises roadshows where you take ex-players out to nights in pubs and clubs for quizzes and questions and answer sessions about football.

"We did a few in Ireland and across Scotland. While we were in Ireland, O'Neill's name came up again and again. When he arrived, everyone was delighted."

Victory after victory in the first few weeks endeared Martin to the legions of hoops supporters, but years of watching their hopes dashed made them nervous even when they were winning.

But gradually, the march towards the championship gained more and more momentum, and this man O'Neill seemed to possess an ability to inspire where others had failed.

Peter said: "Martin seems to be able man manage and inspire the dressing room. He has brought amazing things out of the team. The dressing room is the most important place and he has handled it with great distinction. He seems to get the best out of players in every position.

"He is at ease with Celtic. It seems to be his spiritual home. He has known what they are all about since he was a young lad, understanding what the club is all about and what it means to the fans and the worldwide base.

"Obviously his experience with other clubs have stood him in good stead. He has a lot of humility about him. Every time we have managed to have a chat with him we have been extremely impressed, not just about his knowledge of football but his understanding of the fans and their problems. He manages the club from top to bottom. When we have meetings with him he listens to what we have to say. He has always acknowledged the fans from very early on.

"There's quite a few records may have been broken this year and we are just enjoying ourselves while we can. You can spot a Celtic supporter 500 yards away because of the big smile on his face.

"It is a fantastic achievement and we are hoping for a realistic run in Europe if he can strenghten the team.

"Martin has come and stablised the ship and we can only hope he is there for a long time.

"The team spirit he has created has been fantastic and it shows on the field of play. His skills and ability to bring the best out of every player is quite incredible."

As he has steered Celtic towards glory, it is inevitable that there will be comparisons with the greatest ever Celtic manager the legendary Jock Stein.

Peter added: "People will draw comparisons to Jock Stein and I am sure Martin would be the first to admit there's a bit to go, but you would have to think that he really does have the potential to do tremendous things in management. Let's just hope it is at Celtic.

"He is charismatic character and you only have to look at him on the touchline to see how committed he is.

"We are going to enjoy the closed season and can't wait for next year."

Celtic have always been convinced they have the biggest support in the world, and it seems that every time they score a goal, there are cheers in the other end of the world.

Eddie Toner, general secretary of the Celtic Supporters Associaton said they have 15,000 members worldwide.

"There are supporters clubs from Australia to America, Canada and Europe. I even got a call the other day from a guy wanting to start a club in Kenya. I think we have a fan base of expat Irish and Scots that is second to none.

"The North American Association of Celtic fans have 3,500 people who go and watch every game being beamed back live from Celtic Park. These guys get up at five in the morning and travel 200 miles to watch the game in a pub in places like Boston. That kind of support is hard to beat and I think the club has not really tapped into the support across the world, though with the internet now that is happening."

Like true Celtic fans, they supported them through the lean years. And the arrival of Martin O'Neill has given them hope for the future.

Eddie said: "As a Celtic supporter we lived with the bad times because you either support the club or you don't. The great thing about the fans is that they did stick by the club through the miseries of the 90s and the turmoil that went with that. This season we are getting the rewards that we waited a long time for. You have to support them through the feast and the famine.

"Martin O'Neill came to Celtic on the back of a solid reputation. He was obviously one of the most sought after managers in the game. When he came here at first there was an air of anticipation, but I don't think anyone thought he would turned things around quite so quickly as he has done. Celtic fans would have accepted a bit of consolidation from Martin for a season or two to give him an opportunity to bed in, but what he has achieved this season is beyond all our wildest expectations.

"The fans were happy about his appointment not just because of his solid repuation, but also the fact that he was brought up in the Celtic tradition.

"He's a Celtic man through and through. The bottom line is about someone's ability, but it always helps if someone at the helm shares the same dreams and aspirations as the fans.

"Celtic to us are a unique football club and to have someone in charge who understands that can only be for the best."

The appointment of an Irishman pleased many Celtic fans who foster the Irish traditions of the club.

But the results he produced are more important to fans that being Irish.

Eddie said: "Celtic was founded by an Irishman and the club has a long, proud history from its humble beginnings in helping charitable causes in the East End of Glasgow. But it has moved on from that.

"We have proud links with the Irish and there is an exceptional fan base there. We now reckon that there are about 7,000 season ticket holders in Ireland and that speaks volumes about the committment of people who travel for games.

"During the Fergus McCann period there was talk of bringing down the tricolour and the Bhoys Against Bigotry campaign. Certainly we would never condone bigotry in any shape or form, but there seems to be this feeling in Scotland that being Irish somehow equates to being a bigot, and that is a great disservice to the Irish support. We as an association seek to foster the links between Scotland and Ireland and we are proud of our traditions and history.

"I think part of Martin O'Neill's appeal is not that he is an Irishman but more because he is a Celtic man raised in that tradition.

"Martin O'Neill is working tirelessly for the club and long may it continue. It is early days yet to compare him with Jock Stein, but the comparisons are there. Stein came to the club when it was in turmoil and hadn't won anything.

"He quite quickly turned the club around. Martin came in when the club was probably at its lowest ebb. Last season was probably one of the worst in Celtic's history. To come in and secure the championship and other honours is fantastic, and if he continues to make progress like that then anything is possible.

"He is very approachable. The entire club at the moment has a feel good factor about it and we feel we can approach them on issues that matter to us. He has told us his door is always open."

There is a new confidence at Celtic park, a belief that at last they may have broken through the pain barrier.

Even weeks after the championship fans still get all misty eyed when they talk of that great day.

Eddie said: "It can get very emotional watching important games like when we won the league championship. I was there with my mother and we were both in tears, along with a lot of other Celtic fans. People think back at times like that of when you would go with family as a child. My father used to take me as a child and he died last year, so it was a very emotional moment for me. But that is what the fans are all about - they are like a very large family.

"The scenes of joy after that match were unbelievable. It was different from 1998 when we won, because people are beginning to feel that we are no in at the start of something great. There is such an air of anticipation."

TWENTY TWO

TOM BOYD had just been presented with hunk of silver that represented the massive strides Celtic had taken in the nine months since Martin O'Neill had first entered the gates of Paradise.

The giant SPL trophy was being waved before 60,000 ecstatic supporters, the players danced for joy, hugged each other, wore silly hats and indulged in all the good natured nonsense that one associates with winning a championship.

Standing on the touchline with his arms folded, a smile playing across his features was a man who had seen it all before. More importantly, had done it all before.

John Clark, a Lisbon Lion, and now Celtic's kit man wasn't prepared to join in the celebrations too much.

In a young man's game, he was more than happy to let the young men who had worn the jersey with pride this season get on with it.

Then John Robertson spotted him. The assistant manager isn't exactly backward at coming forward and he was out in the middle giving it laldy when he caught Clark out the corner of his eye.

Within seconds, Clark had been dragged into the middle of the melee and was engulfed and smothered by the players. Clark, a quiet, dignified man, was delighted but so too were the Lions who weren't on the park.

To them, Robertson's actions represented a recognition of their place in the club's history.

In the years running up to Martin O'Neill's appointment, the 11 men who brought the European Cup to Britain for the first time in 1967 had been all but ignored by the club's hierarchy. That was something O'Neill attempted to right within days of joining Celtic.

Over a meal at an Italian restaurant in Newton Mearns on the outskirts of Glasgow, a bond was forged between the man who won a European Cup medal in 1980 and the team that succeeded in the same competition 13 years earlier.

The food was good, the wine flowed but the talk was the highlight of the night and every Lion left the restaurant believing that once again they could feel part of the club they never stopped loving even if that emotion had not been recipocrated by Celtic for many years.

Lisbon Lion Jimmy Johnstone remembers the night and echoes the voices of his team-mates when he paid tribute to the changes O'Neill has overseen on and off the pitch at Celtic Park.

He said: "Martin has brought us back into the club and we have to thank him and Dermot Desmond for that. The first week Martin was there, he asked John Clark if he would get all the Lions together because he wanted to take us for a meal.

"We went to Il Castello in Newton Mearns and we all sat at a big long table and talked football with him. We had a great night and he made a point of spending time with everyone who was there.

"He didn't have to do it but he did, which says everything about the man. He is a great man manager and by the end of that night, WE all wanted to play for him so you can see why the present squad busts a gut for him.

"I see a lot of big Jock Stein in him. Jock made sure you were all right off the field because if you were happy away from the pitch you'd be happy on it. He did that and he was great at it. I think that's what Martin has got as well. He treats people well and they respond.

"Nobody has a bad word to say about him. I've spoken to some of the current players and listening to them, it is obvious he is doing it right.

"I'm not surprised that he's had instant success. He's treated players right and you have to do that with them because they are funny animals. It's difficult to keep them all happy because you can't play them all. That's a tremendous gift in itself.

"They've proved that they've got the ability but maybe in the past they'd been led down the wrong track. That they are back on the right lines is down to the manager.

"The doors are open to the Lions these days. We don't need appointments to come in to see people and that's wonderful because we love the place and sometimes it is nice just to come in and see a few people.

"That's a situation that has changed. The boys are not the type who would be wanting to hang about the place all the time, but it's nice to know that if we ever do pop in then we will be warmly welcomed. It's a great feeling.

"When I saw what John Robertson did on the day the league was won I was delighted. John Clark is the kit man and the job suits him. The players have all got great respect for him because of what he achieved in the game. They think the world of him."

Johnstone, who was not adverse to a bit of crowd entertaining in his time, loves watching O'Neill and his dug-out partners prowling the technical area. He believes the way they wear their heart on their sleeves, celebrating each goal with unashamed delight, has bonded them even closer to the support.

He added: "You know what you can't beat? You can't beat the excitement they show in the dug-out. Some people might say you are the manager of Celtic, so you shouldn't jump up and down, but I don't agree with that.

"You can see how much it means to Martin, John, Steve and the rest of them when Celtic scores. It shows that they care and people feed off of that. It gets the fans going and it is terrific.

"They deserve every accolade but now it's time to go the step further and see if they can deal with Europe. I know Martin will be thinking the same. Europe will be difficult because they will come up against a far better quality of player. But that's where you want to be. You want to be in there with Manchester United and Real Madrid because that's where Celtic should be.

If anybody can do it for Celtic it is Martin O'Neill. And he will."

Johnstone's former team-mate Bertie Auld insists that O'Neill's greatest strength is not giving his players instructions they can't carry out.

The Lisbon Lion said: "The most important thing is that he has got them believing in themselves and he has asked them to do things they are capable of doing. He's not trying to play total football, he is using a system that each and every one of them know they are capable of playing.

"Away from the actual football, the great thing Martin has

achieved is the way he has brought everyone together within the club.

"There is a tremendous atmosphere in there now and he takes the credit for creating that. There is a light-heartedness and a humour about the place that has not been there for years, yet when the players are asked to go out and do their stuff they do it."

The man who wore the number 10 shorts that night in Lisbon's Stadium of Light, added:

"The first thing Martin did was recognise the people that were involved with the club in some of the greatest days in Celtic's history. He acknowledged them right away.

"It doesn't matter how busy he is, as soon as you walk in that door he acknowledges you. It doesn't matter how important make him, he makes you feel important and that is a great quality to have.

"I don't know if we had been shunted to the side before he arrived, but I do know that Fergus McCann didn't really know us. If it started at the top of the tree what was it like at the bottom?

"To be fair to him, he wasn't football-minded. I think the last time he thought about football was when he was born and the nurse skelped him on the arse and said: "Oh, it's a boy - he might play for Celtic.' That was his dream and he never fulfilled it. He had tremendous vision about the stadium but not about the team.

"Martin, though, is a motivator and a football man through and through. I've been a manager myself and I know it is important to get players playing for you. He knows that for anyone to be playing for Celtic they must have ability, but there was something missing. It might have been focus or a willingness to work for each other but whatever it is, he has put it right and turned them into winners. He's given a depth of belief and when they go onto the park they don't think they can lose.

"The Board has given him money to spend and he's spent a goalkeeper, a centre back, a midfield player and a striker. Have a look at all the great coaches and the first thing they do is strengthen the spine of a team – that's what he's done."

Lisbon goalscorer Tommy Gemmell knows O'Neill better than any of his former team-mates. After all, in the twilight of his own playing career at Nottingham Forest, Gemmell played alongside the young Irishman and his fellow Scot John Robertson as they were just beginning to make an impression in England.

The full back with the dynamite in his left boot recalled: "When I arrived at Nottingham Forest, Martin was occasionally playing in the first team with John Robertson. They were both young but clearly had talent.

"I played alongside them both but they played in different positions from the ones they went on to find fame with. John actually played on the right side of midfield and Martin either played centre midfield or up front through the middle.

"The manager was a Scotsman called Matt Gillies and Dave Mackay took over from him. Of course, their careers took off under Brian Clough, but by the time he came to Forest I had gone back to Scotland to finish my career with Dundee.

"Martin was a skilful player and he loved to run with the ball, which was one of our biggest problems! He loved running at defenders but he wouldn't pass the ball. Robbo was the opposite, he loved to knock 40 or 50 yard passes, just knock it around and his job at the time was to build the game for us.

"At that time he didn't take on any players, which was a big difference from how he went on to make his name in the game by playing wide left and running at full backs. It was Cloughie's influence that brought about that change in John's game.

"The effect of them both growing up and coming through the professional ranks together stood them in good stead. They've got a bond and they trust each other implicitly."

Gemmell revealed that he went into Celtic Park early in O'Neill's reign and imparted a piece of advice that the manager clearly took to heart.

He said: "His success has come quicker than I thought. When he arrived at Celtic Park I went in to see him and said: 'Martin, there are only three things you have to do here at Celtic - beat Rangers three times a season. If you do that, you'll win the league because the other results will look after themselves.'

"He went one better than that this season because he beat Rangers four times, including the CIS Cup semi final. He really could not have done any better this season.

"I think he went in with a completely open mind. He said: 'okay, you show me you can do the business for me, and you'll get a game. If you don't do it for me, you are out.'

"Everybody got a fair crack of the whip and he's got the dressing room in the right frame of mind which is extremely important at a football club.

"There is a lot of harmony and a lot of confidence within the club. People want to help each other on and off the pitch.

"Martin's a shrewd wee cookie. He knows what he's doing and

he's served a difficult managerial apprenticeship which has benefited him in the long run. Going from non-league to Wycombe and taking them through the divisions has taught him so much more than any guy who had fast-tracked from playing straight to a big club could experience."

Legendary left winger Bobby Lennox doesn't profess to know Martin as well as Gemmell does but he has noted how O'Neill's players go about their business with a smile on their faces.

He said: "I just think that's because their manager is a great guy. He's very bubbly and his enthusiasm is infectious.

"Martin has been great for the whole club and the Lisbon Lions. When you go to the ground he looks for you and comes to say hello. The whole backroom staff is the same to be fair. Robbo and big Stevie Walford like nothing better than to sit and have a blether with you.

"We are not there on a daily basis but whenever I go into Celtic Park, I see people with smiles on their faces and that is a wonderful thing. There is nothing worse than not fancying going to your work but everybody seems happy there.

"His team is terrific and the boys have been great. No matter how great the manager is, the players still have to do it for you on the park. And they've done it for him all right. They showed what they were all about in the CIS Cup Final when Chris Sutton got sent off and they just got stronger and stronger and went on to win by 3-0.

"The boys at the back have been outstanding, Neil Lennon has come in and played alongside Paul Lambert and they've been great together. Then there's Henrik, who has been just sensational.

"When you meet the supporters they are all smiles. Everyone wants to talk about the Celtic for the right reasons and it makes life worth living doesn't it?

"The second season is always the toughest but I don't need to tell Martin O'Neill that. He's done great and hopefully he will do just as well next season."

Bobby Murdoch, the Lisbon Lion whose sudden death on May 15 cast such a cloud over this season of celebration, spoke just a week before the tragedy of the meeting in the Italian restaurant that told him that Celtic had finally found the right man for the job.

The midfield playmaker said : "Most of the Lisbon Lions have felt for more than the past few years that the club had forgotten about the role we played in its history but the first thing he did when he arrived was get us together for a meal with him.

"We met in an Italian restaurant in Newton Mearns and he spoke to every one of us for a period of time. After that, we were welcomed back into the fold, which has delighted all of us.

"The boys were hurt by what had happened in the past. It was almost as if they were trying to wipe away our achievements. Obviously they had to concentrate on the players they had at that time without always referring to the past, but we all felt that we had made a contribution to the history of the club and didn't deserve to be ignored.

"But Martin realised the feelings that people have for the club and for the team that won the European Cup and he did something about it.

"He comes across as a very intelligent man, he is honest, and what he does on the training ground seems to be getting transferred onto the park which is important.

"That happened with us. We worked hard in training under big Jock and he got the dressing room right. Martin has done that with this Celtic team and everyone benefits if they are all pulling in the same direction.

"Everyone is smiling but that took a long time to come because of how bad the situation was when he arrived at the club.

"There was a bit of turmoil and the fact that Rangers had been so dominant had much to do with that. The club was chopping and changing all the time, not just players but management teams and it was crying out for stability.

"Some players would come for a big wage packet, play for a season then leave under a cloud. That was no good for anybody, but Martin obviously talks to them in a proper manner and he seems to have the knack of making people want to play for him.

"The people I am more pleased for are the supporters. My two boys are 32 and 29 and they haven't seen Celtic win much in their time. I think they get fed up with me going on about the success we had in my time, but now they are happy and they can look forward to more good times.

"He's also chosen his backroom staff very carefully. He trusts them, they are all pals and they work hard together.

"Big Jock more or less did everything himself in our day, although Neilly Mochan and Sean Fallon took us for most of the physical work we did.

"But as far as picking the team and how it would play, that was big Jock's sole responsibility and that will be the same with Martin.

He's got good people around him but he is the boss."

The final word from the Lions has to come from the man who led them. Billy McNeill would certainly win any poll of the greatest ever Celtic player and when he gives his seal of approval it lends genuine authority.

McNeill not only captained the side to the European Cup and to nine league titles in a row, but managed Celtic to the double in the club's centenary year of 1988.

He is extremely happy that the club he loves is again being guided by a man who has a genuine feeling for Celtic.

McNeill said: "Martin has not only recognised the nature of the job but the traditions of the club as well.

"He recognised quickly that he has come to a club that people have an awful lot of feeling for.

"The most important thing for me is that he quickly recognised that he had to organise his first team, get them playing and winning games. That he has done in style.

"I anticipated an improvement but I didn't anticipate such a vast improvement in such a short time.

"I often wondered how Rangers would respond to a strong Celtic team and to be honest, this Celtic team has taken the league apart. They made it their own entirely.

"He took on an enormous job and there are greater benefits in managing Celtic today than there were in the past. The power of the club has been increased dramatically, but nevertheless the job he has done has been absolutely superb and it's quite surprising he has done it in such commendable style.

"Everyone, myself included, is looking forward to see what is going to happen next season.

"The fans are on fire just now and you can understand why when you consider the disappointments they've had in recent times. It's great for them and they are the people who really matter."

Martin O'Neill would probably blush at some of the accolades from the greatest ever Celtic team. But he would surely agree with McNeill's sentiment that bringing a smile to the Celtic support is his greatest gift to the club.

TWENTY THREE

DIDIER AGATHE contests a ball with Ulrik Laursen midway in the Hibs half. The Celtic winger gets the break of the ball and charges goalwards. A split second before a lunging leg tries to disposses him, the Frenchman sends an angled pass into the path of the onrunning Jackie McNamara.

The substitute sprints into the penalty box unchallenged but his first touch takes him wider than he wants so he has to strike his shot with his weaker foot, his left.

It doesn't matter. The ball goes through the legs of desperately backtracking Gary Smith and with goalkeeper Nick Colgan rooted to his spot, it makes it way almost sedately into the left hand corner of the net.

Twenty five thousand supporters packed behind and to either side of the goal, produce a spontaneous explosion of green and white.

They know, as do the players of Hibs, that Celtic are on their way to victory in the 2001 Scottish Cup Final.

Two further goals were added, the first just three minutes after the restart when Henrik Larsson smashed a stunning left foot into the roof of the net and another from the penalty spot with 10 minutes left to cap the club's first Treble in 32 years.

Celtic were certainties in the eyes of the bookmakers in the run up to the final against a team that was pushing against the weight of history.

Hibs hadn't won the Scottish Cup since 1902 – a 99-year wait that becomes more anguished with every passing season. Maybe if Lady Luck is a romantic at heart she will allow the Edinburgh side the chance to win the trophy next season, a century on.

But Saturday, May 26, was the day Martin O'Neill's dream came true. It was the day he completed a Treble that not even the most diehard Celtic fan would have predicted 10 months earlier when the Irishman took the reigns.

Not since 1969 had a Celtic team made a domestic clean sweep in Scotland. In fact, this season's Treble is only the third in the club's 113-year history.

O'Neill watched from the sidelines as his players cavorted on the Hampden turf, milking every second of the celebrations and drinking in the joy that fell like rain from the Hampden stands.

Then one of his players handed him the gleaming old silver trophy. He took it in one hand, held it aloft and marched purposefully from the middle of the pitch towards a corner that was populated with thousands of Celtic fans.

It was a moment that said: 'We've given you this."

But O'Neill knows that in the last 20 years, Celtic's supporters have given the club far more than they've received in return.

There have been moments of passing success. The winning of the double under Billy McNeill in the club's centenary year, for instance. The snatching of the title in 1998, which not only gave Wim Jansen a championship in his one and only season as manager, but deprived Rangers of a record breaking 10-in-a-row title sequence.

But for all the isolated seasons of success there have been many more years of desolation and despair as Celtic lurched from one crisis to the next.

Martin O'Neill has transported those supporters from dismay to delight in less time than anyone would have thought humanly possible.

He has done so by using the memory of the Lisbon Lions as an inspiration, unlike some of his predecessors who have been weighed down by the enormous success the most famous team in Celtic's history enjoyed

On the eve of the final, the manager explained: "I'd never have believed it is more than 30 years since the Treble was won here.

That Celtic side was winning so much, it is surprising they didn't win it more.

"But that team, certainly the 1967, is the greatest ever at Celtic.

"The Lisbon Lions should not be a spectre hanging over us. They should be a driving force.

"We might fall a million miles short but surely to heaven they can drive us on. That team had a fantastic will-to-win - they felt they couldn't lose. We are trying to get that feeling here. We are making progress in that direction."

Of the 48 domestic matches played by Celtic in the course of the season, O'Neill's team lost just three and two of them in the league against Dundee and Kilmarnock occured after the championship had been clinched. That record tends to suggest that Celtic are, indeed, moving in the right direction.

O'Neill's own bosses recognise the fact. The club's main shareholder, Dermot Desmond, perhaps came up with the most eloquent sentence of the season when asked to describe the effect his manager has had on Celtic.

Desmond almost whispered in his soft Irish brogue: "O'Neill has taken ownership of the club mentally."

Those eight words, perhaps more than the millions that have written about the Celtic manager this season, sum up O'Neill's desire to return the club to respectability.

Part one has been achieved with Celtic's conquest of Scotland. Part two involves an assault on Europe.

It might just happen. Honestly, it might. And I really mean that.

SCOTTISH CUP FINAL – MAY 26, 2001
Celtic 3 (McNamara, Larsson 2,) Hibernian 0
Team: Douglas; Valgaeren, Mjallby, Vega; Agathe, Lambert (Boyd), Lennon, Thompson (Johnson), Moravcik (McNamara); Larsson, Sutton